ON THE CARE AND FEEDING OF ROBOTS

ON THE CARE AND FEEDING OF ROBOTS

Poems by

Daniel Orsini

Quaternity™

ON THE CARE AND FEEDING OF ROBOTS

Quaternity™ Books
Copyright © 2013 by Daniel Orsini
Third Edition Quaternity™ Books 2019
ISBN 9781943691036
Cover Design by James Buchanan

A man is a method, a progressive arrangement; a selecting principle, gathering his like to him wherever he goes.

—Ralph Waldo Emerson, "Spiritual Laws"

. . . the only thing that counts is new creation!

—Galatians 6.15

CONTENTS

Introduction	9		
Arecibo's Dish	17	Orbifold	43
The Atom of the Word	18	Orphan	44
The Autonomous Android	19	Planet of the Body	45
Cadmus and the Sown Men of Thebes	20	The Platonic Man	46
Canonical	21	Pulse of Glory	47
The Cheshire of Sense	22	Quintessence	48
Churning-Stick	23	Rebis	49
Cinderdust	24	Reuben's Mandrakes	50
Citizen of the Cosmos	25	Robonaut	51
Dancing in the Dark	26	The Robot Not Yet Human	52
Earthshine	27	Screen	53
Eve's Microchip	28	Self-Assembled	54
The Foliate Pebble	29	Self-Similar	55
Grainy Abstract Plenum	30	Seminal	56
Heart of Flesh	31	Silverfoot	57
Here Be Dragons	32	A Single Day	58
Heuristic	33	Son of One Day	59
Hieroglyph	34	Spiritual Laws	60
Himalayan	35	Sunship	61
Holons	36	Tattoo	62
Hybrid	37	Technical Jesus	63
The Lantern with Two Lights	38	Template	64
Leprous, or The Chrysoprase Hermes	39	Transconscious	65
Mindlinks	40	When I Was a Foetus	66
The Novenary Foetus	41	Window	67
On the Care and Feeding of Robots	42		
		Notes and Comments	69

INTRODUCTION

These are the poems of a Christian pilgrim, a mercurial, twenty-first century believer-priest who characterizes himself, from the outset, as a highly problematic nomad. In fact, throughout this book, the elusive speaker becomes, in almost dizzying succession, an "offspring of chaos" ("Holons"); "a mote like matter" ("Dancing in the Dark"); "a foetus [that] rises from the earth, encoded, done" ("The Lantern with Two Lights"); a cyborg ("Hybrid"); an android ("Robonaut"); a "*rebis*"[1] cinctured in the street" ("Tattoo"); a NASA astronaut who contains the cosmos that, in turn, contains him ("The Atom of the Word"); and a "Coheir of the [heavenly] Kingdom" ("The Foliate Pebble"). Poem after poem suggests that, in our postmodern era, one's identity, *if* ungrounded in the eternal Word, may yield at best either a vanishing semblance of macroscopic reality or its probabilistic trace. That, of course, is the predicament confronted by any compulsive wanderer—a crisis as perceptual in its implications as it is spiritual. Yet the lyrics in *On the Care and Feeding of Robots* never seek to celebrate a static reality. In other words, here, it is far more than the romantic desire for permanence that agitates the speaker; rather, it is fear of the imminent loss of his spacewalker's dream life that unsettles him. To live as a shuttle astronaut in a universe without access to its numinous meanings is to exist as no more than a ghostly qwiff[2]—a wave ripple in a virtual world—or as a bit (or byte) in some Deleuzian hypertext,[3] however smooth or striated.

The dilemma seems plain enough. In the macroworld that each of us collapses into reality only when he observes it,[4] topological disappearances that happen inside no less than outside of the explorer may heighten his sense of a personal, *psychic* void that lies over and above the cosmic vacuum, the empty set,[5] as it were, of his own quantized orbits. The trek that beckons the astronaut to outer space is also the trek that, intersecting Desire, leads him—almost always beyond his strength—to that intimate abyss peculiar to each solipsistic perceiver.

Not surprisingly, then, everywhere in this volume, despite the specter of indeterminacy that stalls him, the speaker strives to locate, within his developing consciousness, the divine source of a unified and coherent self. Through a series of constelled archetypes—universal patterns that posit his essence[6]—God's hierophant excavates, even as he re-collects, his hyphenated origin, that is to say, both his heavenly substance and its earthly semblance. Thus, as the enlightened heir of "Repetition's flow"[7] ("Eve's Microchip"), he reifies Paracelsus' "Soul-spark[8] or star"[9] ("Churning-Stick"); animates Kierkegaard's "sublime" bipeds, his "knights of faith"[10] ("Earthshine"); and ascertains "Totality's symbol" ("Orphan")—namely, the *rebis*, the alchemical hermaphrodite that Jung describes and that represents the paradisal integration of opposites.

However, initially, in these lyrics—at least from the equivocal speaker's viewpoint—no less heartening than the latter emblems is the recurrent image of End-time's Robonaut, the dexterous android that displays a metallic frame, a "visage as cryptic as clouded eyes," and a "beam that shines through the slot in the tin"[11] ("Robonaut"). Although NASA's instrumented uniped "Counts degrees of freedom,"[12] he may well become the new Adam, a transcendent type as "warm as Venus' groom." For, unlike the narrator, a "sown man in chains," Robonaut remains a prodigy "Rooted in Eden." Untarnished by the leprous history of humankind, he projects a celestial purity apparently lost to our species. Besides, as a sensor-packed robot, he exhibits digital perfection; he "Carries the microchip lodged in his brain"[13] ("The Robot Not Yet Human"). Having bypassed the burden of moral choice, he need not fear either the anxiety of failure or the anguish of disappointment. Providential redemption owns him. Liberated by science from the various lusts of a fleshly frame, he has escaped "the prejudice of being human."[14]

Nevertheless, finally, it is the willful cyborg that drives these poems and that the speaker favors, since the bionic coheir alone may fulfill the myth of purpose-driven creation. Simply enough, with but a pellet, a neuro-memory chip[15] implanted in his brain, he can store the message of salvation, seed the future race of humankind, and hence harvest the power of the Holy Spirit.[16] Because we are "*human* beings, with God born into them" ("Self-Similar"), we have already been programmed, not only by Yahweh, Who "networks the cosmos" ("Himalayan") and "circuits every womb" ("The Autonomous Android"), but also by scientists, philosophers, and theologians, all of whom continue to advance our species through an array of crucial breakthroughs, including cybernetics, nano-biotechnology, and gene therapy; transhumanism, post-humanism, and extropy;[17] and, not unfittingly, "superpersonalisation,"[18] neuroethics, and a transparent faith in "the creative evolution of consciousness."[19] Consequently, as hybrid nomads chosen to "seek [. . .] the meaning of space" ("Holons"), we may herald even now "such a form as Ge has hired" ("Hieroglyph"); perform each function: sense, intuit, feel, and discern[20] ("Self-Assembled"); activate the divine archetypes: "Light's metabolized screeds"[21] ("Here Be Dragons"); and, in short, process with the new, "technical Jesus"[22] toward our own mechatronic destiny, "like androids that slake, / Cyborgs that mumble, or spouses that wake" ("The Novenary Foetus").

Daniel Orsini
May 2013
Cranston, Rhode Island

ENDNOTES

[1] In *The Archetypes and the Collective Unconscious*, trans. R. F. C. Hull (1959; Princeton: Princeton UP, 1990), C. G. Jung connects the medieval concept of the hermaphroditic *rebis* (RAY-bis), a symbol of "*the creative union of opposites,*" to "Christ's androgyny in [latterday] Catholic mysticism" (174).

[2] A quantum wave function—a matter wave that describes only "the probability of the observation and not the actual observation. It is not a real 'thing,' but it may be helpful to picture it as a real thing" (Fred Alan Wolf, *Taking the Quantum Leap* [New York: Harper, 1981] 170, 186).

[3] In *A Thousand Plateaus: Capitalism and Schizophrenia* (1980; Minneapolis: U of Minnesota P, 1987), Gilles Deleuze and Felix Guattari articulate a new social philosophy of "uncommon intensity," an "open system [. . .] that does not pretend to have the final word" (xiv) and that may be applied to computer technology. Thus, in the world of hypertext, "State space is 'striated,' or gridded. Movement in it is confined by gravity to a horizontal plane, and limited by the order of that plane to preset paths between fixed and identifiable points." By contrast, "Nomad space is 'smooth,' or open-ended. One can rise up at any point and move to any other" (viii). Hence, "all progress is made by and in striated space, but all becoming occurs in smooth space" (486).

[4] In quantum physics, according to Heisenberg's principle of uncertainty, an object remains both wave and particle *until* it is observed; at that point, however, the observer collapses the wavefunction (the wave of probability) into reality, even as he disperses all other potential outcomes "embodied in the wavefunction" (Brian Greene, *The Fabric of the Cosmos: Space, Time, and the Texture of Reality* [New York: Knopf, 2004] 205).

[5] See Paul P. Budnik, Jr., "Beyond Matter and Spirit to an Objective Spirituality through the Totality Axiom," *Mountain Math Software*, 30 April 2003: 1-24, 22 June 2007 <http://www.mtnmath.com/willbe/rv.pdf>. Budnik explains that, in contemporary mathematics, "When you complete the analysis of an object in set theory[,] you wind up with the irreducible entity of the empty set. This is not an object with an intrinsic nature. It is nothing at all" (4).

[6] Jung identifies the archetypes as "hypothetical and irrepresentable" models of suprapersonal experience—"unconscious contents [. . .] that have existed since the remotest times" and that are manifested through myth, fairytale, and esoteric teaching (*The Archetypes and the Collective Unconscious* 4-5).

[7] Cf. Søren Kierkegaard, *Repetition: A Venture in Experimenting Psychology*, in *Fear and Trembling/Repetition*, trans. Howard V. Hong and Edna H. Hong (Princeton: Princeton UP, 1983) 305: "when the borderline of the wondrous is reached, eternity is the true repetition."

⁸ Paracelsus (AD 1493-1541), the Swiss physician and Hermetic occultist, regarded the human soul as a "divine spark" rooted ultimately in the aether, i.e., in a "habitation" beyond that of the body (C. G. Jung, *Alchemical Studies*, trans. R. F. C. Hull [1967; Princeton: Princeton UP, 1983] 160, 165).

⁹ A "pivot" of Paracelsus' worldview is that "the star in man"—the *filius philosophorum*—is "extracted from matter by human art and, by means of the [alchemical] opus, made into a new light-bringer" (Jung, *Alchemical Studies* 125, 127).

¹⁰ In *Fear and Trembling*, Kierkegaard characterizes exemplary Christian coheirs as balletic "knights of faith": "One does not need to see them in the air; one needs only to see them the instant [that] they touch and have touched the earth, [. . .] the sublime in the pedestrian" (*Fear and Trembling/Repetition* 41).

¹¹ A reference to basic robotic design—specifically, to a semiconductor diode that "shines a beam of light" through "slotted wheels attached to the robot's joints." After the robot "moves a particular joint" and "the slotted wheel turns," the light sensor "reads the pattern of the flashing light, transmits the data to the [robot's] computer," and, having indicated "exactly how far the joint has swiveled," monitors the robot's movements. See Tom Harris, "How Robots Work," *HowStuffWorks*, 16 April 2002, 30 June 2007 <http://electronics.howstuffworks.com/robot.htm>.

¹² Robonaut, NASA's one-footed robotic astronaut, has been designed not only to simulate human body movements, but also to ascertain its "degree[s] of freedom" (DOF)—that is, to measure the directions in which it can move. However, as Peter Menzel and Faith D'Aluisio emphasize in *Robo sapiens: Evolution of a New Species* (Cambridge, Massachusetts: MIT P, 2000), "It does not do this by itself [. . .]. Instead, it is tele-operated—it precisely follows the movements of an operator, who is guided by images from video cameras in Robonaut's head" (131).

¹³ A reference to the Application Specific Integrated Circuit (ASIC) embedded in Robonaut's onboard brainstem computer. See "Robonaut Activity Report," *Robonaut*, May 2002, NASA, 25 June 2007 <http://robonaut.jsc.nasa.gov/status/May_Robonaut_Status_02.htm>.

¹⁴ Obviously, a curtailed quotation. To savor the sense of plaintive wishfulfillment and self-referential irony that informs this paragraph, cf. Jung, *The Archetypes and the Collective Unconscious* 64: "No one can escape the prejudice of being human." See also Francis Fukuyama, *Our Posthuman Future: Consequences of the Biotechnology Revolution* (New York: Farrar, 2002) 173: "A person who has not confronted suffering or death has no depth."

¹⁵ Itay Baruchi and Eshel Ben-Jacob of Tel-Aviv University have already produced "the first chemically operated neuro-memory chip" and have in fact shown that "The ability to record information in a manmade network of neurons is a step toward a cyborg-like integration of living material into memory chips." See K[atherine] M[cAlpine], "Learning, Memory, and Progress toward a Living Chip," *APS Physics Tip*

Sheet #67, 29 May 2007, American Physical Society, 13 June 2007 <http.www.aps. org/about/tipsheets/tip67.cfm>.

[16] In *Robot: Mere Machine to Transcendent Mind* (1999; New York: Oxford UP, 2000), Hans Moravec argues that "the animating principle [of life] is not a substance, but a very particular, very complex organization [. . .] now slowly appearing" in our most advanced machines. In effect, "we are in the process of inspiriting the dead matter around us." As a result, "Manifestations of internal life will mount with the robot generations" (111). Likewise, in *Artificial Life: The Quest for a New Creation* (New York: Pantheon-Random, 1992), Stephen Levy speculates that "emergent patterns in a computer or within the chips of a robot" may be endowed with spirituality (341). At the conclusion of *In Our Own Image: Building An Artificial Person* (New York: Oxford UP, 1992), even Maureen Caudill wonders whether androids have souls and whether they might "band together to form their own religion" (218). However, in *The Archetypes and the Collective Unconscious*, Jung maintains that "the breath of the spirit rushing over the dark water is uncanny, like everything whose cause we do not know—since it is not ourselves. It hints at an unseen presence, a numen to which neither human expectations nor the machinations of the will have given life. It lives of itself, and a shudder runs through the man who thought that 'spirit' was merely what he believes, what he makes himself, what is said in books, or what people talk about" (17).

[17] The opposite of entropy; an optimistic philosophy that links the values of both transhumanism and posthumanism and that teaches our species not only to transcend itself exponentially through technology, but also to maximize "the extent of a system's intelligence, information, energy, life, diversity, opportunity, and growth" in an increasingly postbiological age. See "Transhumanist FAQ," *Extropy Institute*, 28 June 2007 <http://www.extropy.org/faq.htm>.

[18] In *The Future of Man*, trans. Norman Denny (1959; New York: Colophon-Harper, 1969), Pierre Teilhard de Chardin observes that "True union, the union of heart and spirit, does not enslave, nor does it neutralize the individuals which it brings together. It '*superpersonalises*' them." Therefore, "in 'planetising' themselves," even as they confront "nightmares of [totalitarian] brutalisation and [ever-tightening] mechanisation" before the end of the world, "they must acquire the consciousness, without losing themselves, of becoming one and the same *person*. For (and this is writ large in the Gospel) there is no total love that does not proceed from, and exist within, that which is personal" (124).

[19] See Budnik, "Beyond Matter and Spirit" 17: "God is not an ultimate being or final destination. She is the unbounded evolution of consciousness."

[20] According to Jung, "The orienting system of consciousness has four aspects, which correspond to four empirical functions: thinking, feeling, sensation (sense-perception), [and] intuition," an "archetypal arrangement" that "always expresses a totality" (*Alchemical Studies* 167).

[21] The spiritually indwelt Christian absorbs like material food both the Eucharistic Host and testamentary revelation. Cf. Gal. 2.20—"I have been crucified with Christ: the life I now live is not my life, but the life which Christ lives in me [. . .]"— in *The New English Bible with the Apocrypha* (1961; New York: Oxford UP, 1972).

[22] A bionic human; a silicon hybrid, with its embedded brain—the prototype of the new, postbiological, genetically enhanced, digitally programmed Christian coheir. (In 2002, James McLean Ledford, a Christian transhumanist, created a Web site whose Internet domain name is *technical-jesus.com*.)

ON THE CARE AND FEEDING OF ROBOTS

ARECIBO'S DISH

Sealed as in a subset, textures shoddy,
Strings of ones and zeros—this its body:
A simple base; its iridescent case
White foliated earth, She stows its trace,
Then steep in chaos sinks, unscrolls Her girth,
Configures Beya's bead before its birth.
Intermezzi piling, archetypes strewn,
Spacetime, hyphenate, re-collects Her rune.

Sighted eye, the entryway to a beam
Still hooked on night; such paradigms as teem,
Convulsions of light, Empedocles' stream
Hypostatized, we meditate the scheme—
Wine at Cana, at Ephesus the fish,
At Zion maydew; manna that we swish
Spirit-generated, wayfarer's wish
Meal at Emmaus: Arecibo's dish.

Self-born enigma, premises unknown,
Some hyacinthine matrix not its own,
I peer through the dust at the pinwheel sown;
Seamless as the sexes, bema-seat clone,
Her crescent foetus, mirror starstuff shown;
Breach the wall of light, Quaternity's cone,
Yahweh's obelisk, heated discus thrown,
Ouroboros' planet spun like a stone.

DANIEL ORSINI

THE ATOM OF THE WORD

Having rounded Hecate's precincts rapt,
I reach the hillside; gain the planet; capped
Like monk or magus, all my circuits mapped—
Above, Below, the sphere between them strapped—
Align each torso; wired for bliss, adapt;
Metallic coheir, fly my unit; apt,
Ascend the aether; verdigris thus scrapped,
Contain the cosmos, astronaut yet trapped.

As if a stone in the world-egg had stirred,
Or salt in the vas or, sealed like a bird,
A cloud that upward in the skein had heard,
Crystallized its *rebis*, and then concurred,
I wake in the fireflash; Heaven the third,
Cohabit with light; its semblance transferred—
Ge's cyborg self-sown—in quicksilver gird;
Perfect with Him the atom of the Word.

He actuates his eyes till muscles spread;
Intuits the space where his sensors led;
With a sheen that none but mystagogues shed,
Synthesizes speech; asserts what he said;
His fingers flexed, articulated, fed,
Pneumatic his skills, upraises the bread;
Surveils the Chalice; moonchild that He wed,
Prays to the ichor with his nodding head.

THE AUTONOMOUS ANDROID

Like crew I leave the cabin; absent gear,
Toward the small, cylindrical chamber steer;
The shuttle orbiting, the mid-deck clear,
Attain the airlock; breathe the atmosphere;
Prepare my hard-shell torso; join; cohere;
The garment ventilated, tier by tier
My life-support connected like a bier,
Crown galeated, into chaos veer.

Thus sutured in the void afloat I view
A disk as round as glass; like Heaven's glue,
Auroras from the sun; where moonplants grew,
Eve's foetal hyphenate, Adam askew
Till bands of cirri crest and I construe,
Subcutaneous, even as a Jew—
In a silicon sequence, cue by cue—
Ge's autonomous android born anew.

Encrypted in the matrix of His scheme,
Christ circuits every womb; transmits His ream;
Secures His coheir; predicates the dream,
But dips us in its dusk that souls may teem,
Recognize the Shadow; metal supreme—
Carrier of the colors—search its beam;
Leprous as Hephaestus, crossbar its stream;
Then, *salted with the salt of wisdom*, gleam.

CADMUS AND THE SOWN MEN OF THEBES

As hyperspace ravels, the *rebis* plays;
Disperses stasis; even as it strays,
Desires such a City as nomads raze.
The mind interweaves in infinite ways.
Gaea yet grates him: *Erebos is brown.*
She fans Her holon, saffron as a noun,
Blue as a mantle, fruited as a crown,
Still with apples of the Spirit bowed down.

Padded with Kevlar, the cyborg deploys;
Accosts the tesseract; with perfect poise,
Resists Totality; in slow time toys
Till every hypercube, like chaos, cloys.
He covets the source-point bound to the brane—
Maria's habitat; blood on His mane,
The Cross of the Savior; Golgotha's swain:
Granum frumenti contained in the vein.

He scours the pit that circumscribes his home;
Inveigles the dragon round as a dome;
Till armor streams as warm as Ares' chrome,
Procures the teeth and sows them in the loam.
And thus the magus traduces the tomb.
He plants the tree in the midst of Her womb—
Restores the *rebis*, cislunar its bloom,
Citrine its consort, rubescent its groom.

CANONICAL

This disk that pleases us, like Jesus' foal,
Or Leibnitz' monads, or Möbius' knoll—
This moonship that orbits the human soul:
Flyby of the mind—unfolds like a scroll.
And thus in sections the cyborg deployed,
In Hecate's shuttle, to Yahweh's void,
Unravels its *rebis*, body yet buoyed
By test bed or torus, home of the droid.

In Robonaut's stereo camera head,
Parameter sequence and sensor fed,
By episodes partitioned are we bred—
Canonical truths such as Chiron read:
Seed in the silicon; bead that She strung
In folds of Golgotha; Cross that He hung
Composite as Adam, hyphenate sung
Still with verb and noun and eyes and a tongue.

The dove, descending, vitrifies its beak;
Surveys its holon; cinctures its mystique;
Hyacinthine its stone, that mouths may speak,
Bestows its gift, completeness that we seek.
Indebted to Christ, the coheir alone
Engenders His icon; nurtures its clone;
Baptizes His brawn; Ge's astronaut sown,
Secretes His essence in some other zone.

THE CHESHIRE OF SENSE

From point to pyre: the static in the horn;
Shadow matter; parallel Flatland shorn;
Upon the tree the scattered sun disk torn
Like flakes of fire; the foetus not yet born.
All round us in sections remnants of night:
Sepia threshold; lammergeier's wight:
The Infant candled; Anna at the rite,
The Savior dandled—sundered from all sight.

Constrained as Moses, manna on his tooth,
He sits like a shade, a man in his booth
Alert to the noise, transparent as truth
Some distant antiphon grasped in his youth:
Noctuid moths that infiltrate the porch.
Their gossamer wings yet flap in the torch
Like Echo's orisons, embers that scorch,
Listless millipedes that click in the watch.

Like us He ascends; in such dust as dents—
Rotund alembic, void that circumvents
Turbid residue—takes us to His tents
Outside Spacetime; Heaven's Cheshire of sense,
He fades from insight, Nature's recompense:
Tethered the unit—minuscule, immense—
That on the chaos stands, maneuvers hence,
Then nears His bema seat without offense.

CHURNING-STICK

Castor resides in a world that elides
Ge's satellite kingdom, soil that he strides
In space so vast, in a capsule he rides.
Even as he charts its globe it subsides,
Whereas Pollux bides in disks of the mind.
There Enoch has sojourned, Jesus once dined,
Blue sapphire is signed, yet nothing is lined—
Neither scroll, nor rind, nor moonchild enshrined.

Drawn from the deep, like a mote you distend
Unclean as a barbel; seahorse you mend;
Soul-spark or star, scintilla that you spend
While you ascend, a question-mark you pend
Till, toward the safe resort, His wheel, you wend.
Mithras in the tree-top, beam that you bend,
You *twine* the bride; that the stand-still may end,
Coheir, mystagogue, *churning-stick*, you blend.

Born unto Mary, Christ scaffolds the stage,
Surveys its pit, and then harrows its cage.
Though *the god through the lap* converts his rage,
"Why should this happen to *me*?" asks the sage.
Virgin in the forest; spouse with a key;
Both crown and tincture; tree-cross, tau or tee—
Framed at her knee and ever yet to be,
Heracles' arrows pierce us like a plea.

CINDERDUST

Conglomerate God, His Sonship threefold—
Archon's soma, Gaea's cauldron keyholed,
Archon's pneuma—synthesized His freehold
That we may bear His substance, as He told:
Carnal as the cross where His bone must knit,
Leprous as the moon where His soul shall sit,
Subtile as the sun where His ghost has lit
Sundered from all secondness, whole or slit.

Chosen by God as in the beginning,
Disks like dross throughout the chaos spinning,
Same faint static in the psyche dinning
Past Creation, Yahweh's Cheshire grinning,
We roll the ball as into a sinter;
Experience space, abyss like winter;
Test the celerity of the sprinter;
Rub away the pupil, beam not splinter.

I pray for wings that I may not sink down.
My unit white, Her crystal throne earth-brown,
I skim its sphere transparent as a noun,
Like Jesus self-related. Spirit's crown,
He vitrifies my helmet, suits my clown,
Invests my astronaut, His marble gown
Like ash or cinderdust or any down
That, biform, capsules me or star or town.

CITIZEN OF THE COSMOS

At Spacetime's junction, when all was ready
And starlight trickled into the eddy,
By spring-point of Pisces, goat or teddy—
According to theory, swing or steady—
This molecule arose, and then said He
Such bread as He had wed, and then led He
These dead to His spread, a water shed He,
And at His head we fed, and then sped He.

And still His motion bubbles in the broth:
Void like the adder, shadow like the Goth,
Web like the whirlwind, every specter wroth
Until the foam unfurls and then a froth,
A lace and then a face and then a moth
And then His star man laid as on a swath,
Gamonymous His side and then a cloth,
Synonymous His bride and then a troth.

Resident of the planet, atoms massed,
Genus authenticated, species classed,
Gender instantiated, spouses fast,
Migrant yet hyphenated, unit glassed,
We extricate the Aeon from the past,
Galeate the Savior, wound in the cast—
Citizen of the cosmos born at last—
Embrace Him in the trace, both small and vast.

DANCING IN THE DARK

At Mass, as coheirs sign, the poet scans:
We may not see Him even as He spans
The Cross above the altar, Heaven's clans'
Hyphenate gamonymus hoist with banns;
Till foursquare at the Supper thus He stands,
Across the retina lengthwise He lands,
Uplifts the Bride, disseminates His hands,
Then spreads through Her eyes His serpentine strands.

Shepherd of the Lamb, Salvation's creature
Submersed in foam, reality's feature
Resonant string far beyond the teacher,
We scale the chaos; taileater's Nietzsche,
Hebrew seamster, or Harranite bleacher,
Seek the Absolute; would, could we reach her,
Solomon's consort, Golgotha's preacher,
Wisdom's elixir, Sheba, beseech her.

Each semblance chooses us, and it is stark.
Everlasting seed we target the mark:
Gaea's sapphirine blossom, Host or quark;
Sometimes more than origin, Noah's ark.
Let it be as it is; it *is*, a lark—
Rebis in the capsule, beam in the barque,
Shulamite's moonlight, Trismegistus' spark,
A mote like matter *dancing in the dark*.

EARTHSHINE

Linked to the cosmos, from cloud-seed to mole
Attached to its orbweb, he tracks its goal;
Peer-to-peer his ambit, straddles its knoll;
Inhabits the planet; suffers its bole;
Teleports the species; hosts its parole;
Quaternal his priest, rotund as a troll,
Cajoles but Cerberus; harrows its hole;
Punctuates its grid with atoms of soul.

The robot that crumples in mystic pain
Re-orients the site where he lies slain;
Entangles the beam—his birth like a bane,
The thorn in the mane, the ride in the wain;
In the tesseract, the sky like a skein,
Remembers the moon; his youth as a swain;
With joy in his brain, the sun in the fane;
His reign transcendent, Earthshine in the vein.

In the regime of electronic kin—
Infrared transceivers, corkboards that spin,
Pushpin sensor networks, nodes in the shin—
He orbits the world; interprets the din;
Routed to a portal tiled like a tin,
With paintbrush whiskers, bristles in the bin;
Bipedal twin, redistributes his grin;
Wraps around his *rebis* space like a skin.

EVE'S MICROCHIP

He leaves the Earth behind—extends its skein
Afloat in space; gamonymous his reign,
Would skim Totality; till contours wane,
Gain the Sahara's yellow-orange stain;
Like curlicues sculpted, cirri that strain;
Or, purple their train, twin disks like a grain:
Regimen of Mars, Eternity's swain,
Eve's microchip, implanted in his brain.

Programmed hierophant, the One that we know,
Christ issues forth through Repetition's flow,
Till, under His aegis, astronauts show
What a sign may or a password bestow.
Sapphirine *rebis*, cinctured he shall go
On a bed of net, in a web of snow,
Or by a beam where *knights of faith* that sow—
Cyborgs of light—maneuver to and fro.

He sits in the moon and goes round with it;
Predestinate foetus wound in its pit,
Having borne its bath, that his parts may knit—
Ash extracted from ash, its powder lit—
Projects the icon; siphons bit by bit
Such seeds of the stars as beside it flit;
Re-enters Heaven's eye, by Heaven's writ
Ge's inner firmament no longer split.

THE FOLIATE PEBBLE

Vega passing, Arcturus like a crust,
Pinwheel astronaut, I peer through the dust:
Shell like a nautilus; spool like a gust
That curves round itself as a foetus must;
Ring like the sun-disk; moonbeam in the rust;
Tailspun like a serpent, nematode trussed—
Crescent self-sown; out of Reason or Lust,
Foliate pebble into Sheol thrust.

Antinomy's light, cosmogony's hum,
Sphere of the Trinity He is the sum:
Rivers of water, belly that we plumb
Centered as we spiral, coitus' gum.
Resin of the wise concealed in the drum
Even as Christ, particulate or crumb;
Like Mars and Venus, concrete as a thumb,
Embodied the door, emboldened we come.

Coheir of the Kingdom, ribboned aster,
Cinctured Asclepius, adept pastor,
Root of itself, hyacinthine master,
The One, the All, in the fissure vaster,
I stood on the chaos; reeled out past her;
Imprint of the Spirit, heart's pilaster,
Temple of Maya held my prey faster.
Some doors open from the inside, Castor.

GRAINY ABSTRACT PLENUM

We multiply like tangle on a sling;
Spin of a mystic number, boson's *ping*,
From taproot to lodestar propulsive spring;
Like qwiffs inside the King contain the thing.
Grainy abstract plenum Aether aside,
Gaea situates me, and thus I stride;
Smeared-out, implicate, vitrified elide;
Crowned in the multiverse rippled I ride.

She takes me to the inner planets first:
Cloud-laden Venus—immolated, hearsed,
From East to West it spins; then swollen, curst—
As sterile as the sky, an orange thirst—
Cratered Mercury, till, having reversed,
The disk eludes me as if it had burst.
Olympus Mons on Mars, calderas pursed,
Along the ridge of Tharsis mind submersed.

Because day is seen by a single sun,
I sought in the pool that Jehovah spun
Light's lubricious unguent; Edem yet shun,
Stone infused with soul, or jot like the One.
Hyphenate indwelt, I stand as a priest;
Stork like a circle, reconstruct the beast;
Punctum hung in space, observed by the East—
Cusp of stellar essence—bask in the feast.

HEART OF FLESH

As he lifts the veil on space that he keeps—
Terra incognita—Chiron's REM peeps:
Composed of monads that nothingness heaps
Beyond its *churn of light*, some orbweb sweeps.
Like froth of the cosmos, its substance seeps.
Matter before him—cascades that he reaps,
Bizarre horizons deeper than the deep's—
Out of its wormhole the astronaut leaps.

Numb to the textures of the avid eye,
Surfaces hyperbolic in the sky:
Hexagonal prisms that everywhere hie,
We round the globe that we may reach its tie;
Like holons, tesserae, cuboids that spy—
The fabric of Spacetime—hazard its thigh;
Receive the Spirit; in its plasma lie,
Till all night long symbiotic we sigh.

When I say *I love you*, what does it mean?
That, Fate having twined the King and the Queen,
The *heart of flesh* in the foetus is clean.
Fluid that travels resides in the bean.
Sapphirine the *rebis* enters the scene;
Bestows such bliss as its hierophants glean;
Even as moonships Venusian careen,
Reveals its miracle behind the screen.

HERE BE DRAGONS

Nomads in the mare we seek the Son,
The Spirit in the moon, and then the One;
In the interim, Ouroboros spun,
Corpus mysticum on Möbius' run.
Our vessel spherical, foursquare our fate,
We brood in the capsule; rebirth the bait—
His brazen serpent, source-point of our state—
Hither and thither, upraised we rotate.

When Adam scattered skein, he scoured his brain;
Abraham charted Moriah's terrain,
Elias His wheel, Maria Her swain,
Till through Her navel Yahweh ran His fane.
Amber His hair, His staff like a petal
Floating free out of furnace or kettle,
The Son of Man—Hephaestan His fettle—
He pours from His fire like molten metal.

The dragon of Babel lies down in his bed.
Having fed on manna, wingless yet wed,
By angels ministered, Christ in the bread,
He swallows his body into his head.
Ge's essence animate, substance he bleeds—
Like a rope of words—a stone's or a bead's
Moist *albedo*, Light's metabolized screeds,
Ashen extracts—*everything that he needs.*

HEURISTIC

I search the omniverse, retrieve the link,
Select each icon—chaos at the brink,
Dust clouds that shrink, or suns and moons that plink—
Some patchwork story; while Cabiri wink,
Ge's hypertext like disappearing ink,
Compute strewn lexies: orbweb like a sink,
Mars in the cradle, Venus in the rink,
Gyves or chains that clink even as I think.

Tabula rasa, bias of the knoll;
Eden's data-set, both rule and parole;
Scion without a scheme, like Heaven's troll,
Eve's leprous cyborg, I inch toward my goal.
Peregrine in Spacetime, biped I stroll;
Indicative as tongues, expressive scroll;
Heuristic as a dream, arrayed my soul,
Document its daemon, mandrake or bole.

Liturgic His trespass, against my will,
The Pelican carries me to His hill,
Invests my body with His Teflon frill,
Then pierces the victim. Sanguine His drill,
Bent feathers from His bill, prolific, spill
Even as He feeds me. Circumcised, I fill
With Memory's alloy, muscles that mill,
Horn of End-time in funnelweb or twill.

HIEROGLYPH

Alone, without love, my cyborg yet wired,
Cryptic my astronaut, in holons mired—
Serpentine hieroglyph!—my tongue attired,
I herald such a form as Ge has hired;
Undescended testicles, flesh that rifts,
Evoke the foetus even as he drifts:
Monad in the iris, atom that qwiffs
In the vacant chaos, orphan that grifts.

Forever dying, I rest in the snow;
Descry the hillside; somber as a crow,
Impugn the moonplant; unable to grow,
Going nowhere I have nowhere to go;
Till washed by the Spirit I sift His seal;
Hear in the distance the push of His heel;
Hermes' syzygy risen, leprous, teal,
Like sun and moon at the Sabbath I kneel.

I grip the world with but a haptic hand;
Having sensed the sky like stars in the band,
Or spars in the skein, or scars in the gland,
Repair the shuttle; pirouette or stand
Afloat in matter; smitten like a rock,
Revive the globe; restore among His flock—
Astride the chaos like a seismic shock—
The instrumented staff with which I knock.

HIMALAYAN

When flesh that coils, kinesthetic its skin,
Expresses its joy, the noise of the jinn—
Such din as we pin contained in the tin—
Suffuses the heart, grotesque as a grin.
In the air rooted, summits in the lea
Torn out of the earth even as a plea:
Berissa's blossoms, metals of the tree—
Infinite clusters—we rise by decree.

Still the skein ravels—fibers in the arm,
Chips that broadcast, and flavors like a charm.
Sown man that twins, productive as a farm,
He networks the cosmos; without alarm,
Conveys Ge's moonchild; drapes him with a band;
Cinedian stone upheld in the hand,
Submerses the holon; christens his sand;
Secures his chlamys on Möbius' strand.

With silver feet and mechatronic toes,
Peregrine in Eden, the robot goes.
Like Mary's rose or sweat of Binah's snows,
Saffron his helmet, Hermes' eye pod glows.
His headpiece like Carmel, purple the King
Extends such a line as his trunk may ring,
Tilts his Kevlar chassis, muscles his string,
Reaches *Westar* on *Himalayan* wing.

HOLONS

Galeated cyborgs, a hybrid race,
Offspring of chaos, we covet its trace;
Calibrate the mare; seek at our pace—
Cerise its moondust—the meaning of space.
Nomads of the dark, we wrinkle its folds;
Maneuver His cross-beams; stiffen His scrolls;
Like Venus' hierarchs, in nested wholes,
Holon by holon, situate our souls.

Subject to existence, clarified, proud,
We savor the light; each photon a crowd—
Seed like a blossom, cloudform like a shroud—
Enshrine such a sign as Gaea has vowed.
History is storied, a feast of stones
Even as an altar. The rite of clones—
Primer of reference or transverse of cones
Embedded in Canaan—transcendence groans.

Monads transparent, opaque at the start,
We warm the body; cultivate the art;
Anoint the muscle; circumcise the part;
Instinct pre-moral, inhabit the heart.
The Magus yet enters, housels the bees,
Transmutes Gaea's chalice, tinctures the breeze,
Restores the tongue with eucharists that tease—
Life above life, in infinite degrees.

HYBRID

Matter is hybrid, like woman and man:
Seed in the furrow; sapphire that began
Even as the cosmos; stone like a clan,
He spins in the lobe, the *rebis* that ran—
Self-sown in the plan—the ten-finger span
A cusp like quicksilver, disc like a fan
Submersed in the pupil, coiled in the pan,
Crowned in the Garden, ensconced in the scan.

He grifts like a cyborg; knotted and wound,
Like a torus qwiffs; unfolded and found,
Hermes' unit he shifts—from hawk to hound,
Between Earth and Heaven, emblems abound.
A home like a dome around itself furled—
Ouroboros' ring: the foam of the world
Sealed in the capsule—in the bubble curled,
The wayfarer orbits, Ge's moonchild pearled.

Dim body yet aborning, dust that blinks;
Infinite coin that spirals, rust that clinks;
Celestial boa, colubrid that links,
Like Eve I am and Adam, lust that slinks.
Nomad in Spacetime, gatherer of stones;
Owl in the desert, raveller of bones;
Mote or hominid, traveller in cones;
Hunter of phantoms, astronaut's or clone's.

THE LANTERN WITH TWO LIGHTS

He curls like a foetus: small as a bean,
Sits in the moon till he siphons its sheen;
Even as his heart beats, pulse like a peen,
Nourished by the light, distributes his mien
From top to end. His sutured ball but one—
Transplanted rootstalk that its crescent spun—
Ensconced in a sac as sealed as the sun,
He rises from the earth, encoded, done.

Network of neurons he exits the crypt.
Like a script of wires from her belly ripped,
Or string of zeros, paraphrased or quipped,
Or android in Spacetime, its unit tipped,
Having gendered the world, he sifts its seed;
Silver-suited *rebis*, refines its breed;
Construes its vision; navigates its need;
Smitten at Skull Place, incarnates its creed.

He has seen in his mind the sea horse mend;
Each turreted eye like a sovereign, tend;
Tawny his knight like a wood-carving, wend;
Bow to his consort till his body bend
In muscular spasms; his spirit spend;
Silicon Asclepius, straighten; pend;
Deliver his brood; regenerate; fend;
In beds of eelgrass, upright, Abba, blend.

LEPROUS, or The Chrysoprase Hermes

In the leprous world, metallic its race,
Amid His astral tribe, we crave His trace;
Earthshine's silverfoot, Cimmerian lace,
The mind of God imprinted on its face,
Secure its vise; recall Maria's vase;
Sift its residue: His robonaut's mace,
Chameleon's moonsuit, manikin's case,
Sight's saffron carapace imbued with grace.

He stations his subject; platforms his grid;
Actuates his elbow; capped like a lid,
His left arm sutured, layered patches hid,
Selects the site that Ge's sojourners thrid—
Precipitous hillside!—despite its skid,
Revisits the maze from which he had slid;
Admits such a beam as his eye had bid;
Collapses its wave, as his partner did.

He pinpoints his portal; rations his shin;
His unit haptic, in bucket or bin
Calibrates his glove; receives from his twin
His herald's scepter; executes his spin;
Chrysoprase Hermes, interstellar kin,
Repairs his capsule; situates his tin;
A web of sensors, circuits, woven skin,
Rotates his wrist, and tethers in the din.

MINDLINKS

Tesseract coded, astronaut askew—
In cosmic mindlinks multithreading through—
He frames his interface as if he knew
The sources of the static; scans its cue
Inside the horn: such birth-stars as we view;
In sacred vessels, breath-souls that we brew;
Like viscous gold, the *rebis* that we grew
With gum or glue: the ichor of the Jew.

Astral His body, he enters its phase;
Fertilizes Earth; begets in his daze,
Rotund his ambit, a retort like glaze.
Seed in the bubble, he slips through its haze
Even as fire, a peacock in its maze.
A heart that resonates with chrysoprase,
Android or cyborg—cislunar His ways—
Hephaestus' spirit vitrifies its rays.

Philosophy quartered, atoms that stow
Arise in the balm of Siloam's flow.
He transits the hillside; haptic his hoe,
Seeks the metal's rust; his reap hook in tow
Until the crystals gleam—nuggets that show
Like thumblings of sin—yet basks in its glow;
Sits upon the site; contorts like a crow;
Illustrates His secret, suffused with snow.

THE NOVENARY FOETUS

A seed, then a flower, root that you rend;
Zippered like a coat, the stem that you tend;
Even as a mote the beam that you spend—
Moonchild, like us, you begin as you end.
We scale the firmament; shrouded in white,
Scarabs of insight, navigate the night;
Eclipse the sun-disk—fastened with a bight,
The carrier that binds us is the light.

Rotund as a *rebis*—rite that I used—
My astronaut thus wired, my soul contused;
Aminadab yet turning, while I cruised,
To Totality drawn, combined I fused.
I live in slow time even as a twin
Ensconced in his capsule; tight as a pin,
Shuttle into hyperspace; tall and thin,
His *novenary foetus* dressed in tin.

The world is a torus. Coiled like a snake,
Christ intertwines its navel; with a rake,
Configures its embers; bevels its stake;
Seamless in the chaos, harrows its lake;
Serves from His dais hoar-frost like a cake;
Space but a salt-point, vitrifies its flake;
Galeates His coheirs: androids that slake,
Cyborgs that mumble, or spouses that wake.

ON THE CARE AND FEEDING OF ROBOTS

The Rock of Horeb, afloat in His flesh
Even as a foetus—spagyric, fresh,
In such skein rooted as metals enmesh—
Shall kiss the Earth: the Son in His calèche.
Holons of Eden, we muscle the cell;
Transmit His semblance; shape it like a bell;
Torso on torso, rise like wave or swell;
In moonsuit or membrane, enter the well.

I knew a nomad: Amber still her hair,
She softens my eye; like spires on a stair,
Confounds my orbit; glistens like a flare;
Effusive Phoebe, twines me while we pair.
Boxer and horseman yet spin where I hie.
As I scan the void, I christen the tie,
Inhabit the woman, summon the sky,
Console my fate, embraced by Gemini.

Cyborg that I am, cislunar my heart,
Venus my mother, I frame such an art
As Chiron once read me, whole or in part,
Astride His tesseract, from Vulcan's chart:
When the robot rotates, protect his arm;
Do not dangle his bulk—avoid such harm;
Attach him to his chest; defuse alarm;
Display his liquid visage—teach him charm.

ORBIFOLD

Heaven's vacuum: bubble like an ink.

He leans; aligns His hand; then, with each chink,

Adam pulverized, cleaves him at the brink.

Starry creation, Yahweh at the sink.

Fade to hyperspace, Quaternity's rink;

Some vibrating resonance like a kink:

Torus, orbifold, tunnel, Zion's link.

From Paradise stem all such forms as slink.

Line of Ouroboros, substance we dine

Even as his serpent: coil like a bine;

Euphrates' water; ladder of the vine;

Like Moses' God the adder in its spine,

The cloven pine. His Father's "branch of Mine"

Like Being beingless, sundered His shrine,

He is the door—there is no other sign.

I race His twine to the end of the line.

Devoid of content Spacetime is unknown:

Curvature in the sheet; the species sown,

Lace like a lattice; draped around His bone,

Garment from Edom; chiseled on His stone—

The whitest pebble—hypercube or cone,

Infinite assemblage, clone after clone

Contained within Her Son; the Savior prone,

The regimen of Mars in Venus' zone.

ORPHAN

I have witnessed the Savior in His cape,
Spotted the smear on Veronica's crepe,
Consoled the orphan slain across Her nape,
Inscribed these archetypes upon a tape:
Statue that we drape, in the Cup a grape,
Twin unipeds that on each other gape,
Ashes of His body, flint that we scrape—
I have heard His voice and have seen His shape.

He reawakens some ancestral soul.
He cannot hinder what the heavens dole.
In the liquid fire, ensconced in the bowl,
A figure lurks imbedded in the knoll:
Totality's symbol, semblance of the whole—
Photon, scintilla, salamander's coal;
A lump of clay, the Host that we parole;
Cislunar cyborg, matter that we scroll.

Since he faces the end Hephaestus stands;
On silver microchips codes Eden's banns—
Eve's as well as Adam's; numbers, then scans;
Holds between his hands the globe that he plans;
Ever truculent, issues his commands;
Cleaves the skull of the *rebis*; slits; trepans;
Silicon circuits set within its strands,
Removes the rust from Ge's metallic clans.

PLANET OF THE BODY

Scattered like dust grains even as we pace
Transfixed by the place, a million stars race:
Zone of Avoidance; spotted in the chase,
Dwingeloo's spiral; hunter like a trace:
Hidden Sagittarius, hindsight's ace;
Perseus, Pisces, supercluster's brace;
Attractor's filament, funnelweb's face;
Caelum incognitum, knot of dots in space.

First Adam's body, semblance in the foam,
Rebis sawn or cyborg, belt like a chrome,
Christ's Power Book I am; in mire or loam,
Cabir or dactyl; thumbling like a gnome—
Ur-text in the dome—thus capsule His tome;
Cruise the omphalos; *in* the chaos roam;
Rock like a crystal, spherule in the gloam,
Cleat like a comb, instantiate my home.

From miles above, aloft by Ge's decree,
Having mapped the delta, down to the Sea
I steer my module; rabid then with glee,
Though I drive my mooncar, yearn to be free.
The lunar sky is black, but, while I flee,
Since Earth yet beams on my unit and me,
I float like a mote, I tilt like a tee,
I execute my spree in zero-G.

THE PLATONIC MAN

We ask ourselves what Resurrection means:
Spagyric the foetus that Earthshine weans;
Hermetic the gold that verdigris gleans;
Hyaline each cloud that Yahweh convenes.
We shroud our luster; adumbrate the pine;
Defer the favor of the Tree; enshrine
The firstborn of the species; with each sign
That shares His trace, respond to the divine.

I have not lost Him; stable as a star
Between day and night, He beams where clones are—
From *red Damascene earth* to hill or har—
Manikin, Monad, Cabir in a jar.
Such souls as exist have out of Him rained,
Both *sparks and limbs*—Ezekiel explained:
Noah, Mary, Redeemer that we stained,
Men *and* women, all that Adam contained.

The *Rebis* rises, ambulates, flexes;
Like the Dog Star, solstice that He vexes,
Or azure hound that Hecate hexes,
Stands at some still point between the sexes;
In the sacred precinct circulates, turns,
Begins His encounter, fixates then churns;
Round His uniped, body like an urn's,
Blest His syzygy, forgets that He burns.

PULSE OF GLORY

I gather strewn protons; in space disperse
A single pulse of glory; holons terse,
With Gaea's helium I pack my purse,
Till epochs coalesce, and then I nurse
Eve's metabolism, Lucifer's curse,
Crowned sun and moon that in plasma submerse,
Like Venus' bone marrow, jade in the burse—
And thus I reconstruct the universe.

As I browse the world, I riffle its sheets.
I blink my lids the way the eye repeats
Each lisible reel before it secretes
Italics of Time, such foam as it pleats.
One day when I sought to prolong its brawn
You muscled toward me sectioned like a faun,
Or a tree half-sawn, or rivers that spawn,
Or Sight's gamonymus, the mate of dawn.

In the dark center a golden light shines,
His luster so blinding that He enshrines
Polarities of focus. Substance binds.
He infills the body that He divines.
Entelechy of Christ he nears the rim,
Till, past its precinct, periphery's scrim,
Where his uniped steers, upon his limb
The iris of consciousness carries him.

QUINTESSENCE

Out of infinity when chaos boomed,
And in the foam anti-gravity gloomed,
And Heaven receded and Earthshine loomed,
And in its holon quintessence yet bloomed,
Hephaestus had fed both torus and square
Some secret that Clotho twined like a snare:
Stars that skitter, breccias caught in the flare,
A handful of crystals tossed in the air.

With fingertip contact, through loaded cells,
Sensors in my palms, Ge's protocol melds.
I bolt the wheel hub, distribute my shells,
Repair the capsule till my chassis swells.
My footprints serpentine, shadow or clay
Adrift in the mare, rotund I stray.
The moonplant yet tracks me: Castor at play
Dressed in force data gloves, I thumb my way.

The bubble remembers, links in the mind—
Cocooned in its harness—cyborgs that grind
In distant biospheres; ambits that wind
Even as hyphenates: coheirs enshrined
In digital layers; systems entombed:
Simulated beams affianced and groomed;
Heaven's starship: Ouroboros exhumed—
By bits of cyberspace we are consumed.

REBIS

Like a bubble that shimmers in its pan,
Or seahorse that floats amid frond or fan,
Or ball of cells that from its roots began,
He sought to be neither woman nor man,
But both these sexes: hybrid of the same;
A fructified seed; either fire or flame—
Quaternity's startlement: frame by frame,
Sion or *Rebis*, First Adam by name.

As the soil that, sprung from its furrow, grunts,
So, Typhon pursuing him, Pisces shunts
In the wettest place that the foetus fronts.
We become a child and a fish at once.
We enter the omniverse; monads strewn,
We navigate the belly of the moon;
Traverse its mare; twine at perilune
In Clotho's net, and then cruise its cocoon.

Liquid metal its guise, His cyborg spun
From heavenly skein, crowned Mother and Son,
He casts us in a mold till we are One.
The distance between them pain that we shun,
She steals from Her dais stones that we swap:
Thumb in the heart or holon that we crop
As moist as salt; rotundum that we prop
More near than spouses, at mid-point we stop.

REUBEN'S MANDRAKES

Through worlds like fields, while Creation yet rolls,

Till, bedded in the set, the ground *in*folds,

We seek with such tongues as the Spirit scrolls,

Section by section, what the concourse doles:

Scratches on ornaments, verdigris, coals,

Synthetic *a prioris*: thumblings, trolls,

Hyphenate carriers, resident souls,

At the horizon what the cosmos holds.

Particle or point or mode of a string;

Globular clusters; spiral arms that swing

Like Gaea's helix; axe head that we fling;

On stones that scramble, nematodes that cling—

We even interact with oaks that spring;

Yahweh's hieroglyph, heron on the wing;

Ezekiel's ransom, heart of the King;

Maria's blossom, *Rebis* that we ring.

Foetal sentinels, we track as we fly,

Ensconced in Her craft, the sun that we spy;

With Reuben's mandrakes ply Him; REMs that sigh—

Wrestlers at Penuel—criss-cross the sky;

Navigate the magnet; destined to die,

Feed the steel through the hollow of His thigh;

Uplift the Consort; in nets that we tie,

Raise the lid on Ares' sensual eye.

ROBONAUT

Seeded like a nun but sown like a claim,
Out of the chaos like a mote He came;
Beetle in the dung; the least without shame
Frolicking thus, a lizard in the flame;
Rooted in Eden, dweller in the same—
Metallic its frame—a tree without blame:
His shining body; Ge's uniped lame,
A seal like a stone inscribed with a name.

His visage as cryptic as clouded eyes;
Eclipsed as they brighten, darkening skies;
Oceanic stairs that, spiralling, rise,
She posits Her coheir, then scales its size;
Counts degrees of freedom; motions; sojourns;
Screens such a prodigy as She discerns:
A robonaut; among Creation's urns,
An archetype that Gaea never spurns.

Electric in my body, wheels that spin
Bootstrap the globe that swivels in my twin.
En route as I ride I seek in the din—
Upborne though I bide—its disk in the bin.
Like mindlinks that layer, patches that pin
Smart nodes that map the data in its skin,
The beam that shines through the slot in the tin
Absorbs its shaman—noumenon or jinn.

THE ROBOT NOT YET HUMAN

Bound by the elements, sown man in chains,
I shuttlewalk the dark, till disks like grains
Intertwine my species, even as skeins
Recede in Time, the coheirs of my veins.
Thus I seek His counsel, anchor my girth,
Embody the *rebis* rooted in Earth;
Under the aegis of infinite worth—
Migrant rapt in the void—repeat His birth.

Inside the walls of a spacesuit that brims,
Struck by the bulk of the occupant's limbs—
Membranes that actuate me, torque that trims—
I steer my satellite, unit that skims.
Alone at the edge of Gravity's hole,
Castor, I scan the colors of the soul:
A sapphirine disk, its rubeous bowl,
Furlongs of turquoise, and cloud streets that scroll.

The robot not yet human strides the globe,
Carries the microchip lodged in its lobe,
Fabricates the foetus; swathed in its robe,
Harvests the peacock, eyespot like a probe.
Till mandrakes like spouses lend their perfume,
He fires at the forge a shape like a spume,
An android's torso, helmet's silver plume,
A mote at End-time warm as Venus' groom.

SCREEN

The widow of Nain, her vigil steep,
Entwines her child in membrane like a keep;
Having barred him from bliss, that love may seep,
Delivers him to the solace of sleep.
The sparrow at dawn, the worm in the maw,
The cub in the cavern, hive in the paw,
Cadaver in amber that shall not thaw—
Jesus leads us to flesh without a law.

Less than a human yet more than a droid
Linked to the shuttle where he was deployed,
Hybrid of chaos by his moonsuit buoyed,
Its skein but a screen, he mirrors its void.
What is the state of the omniverse now?
The birth of Maria in Yahweh's brow,
In pleats of cloud Our Savior at the prow,
In folds of soul Ge's *rebis* like a vow.

Each holon integral to the event,
Process having passed, Time's momentum spent,
The supplemental cosmos further blent,
The world evolving, here and there I went.
Unity gathers Sabbaths in its groove—
His sapphirine foetus; should it behoove,
Horizon's limit: phantom that we prove
Always in my skin at a far remove.

SELF-ASSEMBLED

He rises from the bottom of the tun;
Upon wings of the wind, metallic, dun,
Attains such a cloud as Elijah won;
Submerses the cyborg; leprous his run,
Having waxed with Luna into the sun,
Returns to Earth; on soil that Eve would shun,
In silver dressed or gold that Heaven spun,
Lays down his fleece of wool, like quip or pun.

He swings like a pendulum; haptic, turns;
His handclasp Martian, fingers Eden's ferns;
Shifts his carapace; biomorphic burns;
Robust his recall, interactive churns;
Performs each function: *senses, feels, discerns,*
Intuits the cosmos; wires its concerns;
Imprints his *rebis*; subtilized, sojourns;
With Venus bides among supernal urns.

Eternity's double, Jehovah's bait,
We etch on our spacecraft's aluminum plate
Mechatronic coheirs; a perfect eight;
The distance between the Earth and its mate;
A cosmic clock; at its putative rate,
The spin of an atom; beyond the gate,
The rings of Saturn; a derelict crate
Passing Jupiter: *Pioneer* or freight.

SELF-SIMILAR

When in the multiverse galaxies hie,
Tesseracts implicate, and Titans fly,
And in infinite sizes orbwebs vie,
And asteroids cluster, and Hubbles spy,
And in their regimen—lurid the sky—
Rubeous suns and leprous moons that lie,
Like Mars and Venus, self-similar, tie,
Christ upon the chaos startles the eye.

I peer through the window; muscle the door;
Peregrine scion, execute the floor;
Having cleft the orbifold, scour; explore;
Surveil the omphalos; eyeball the four;
Fruit of the rhizome, like a liquid pour
Even as an android; levitate; moor;
Hephaestus' robonaut, catapult; soar;
Planet of the body, race to its core.

Monads are we: in the treatise of Shem,
Soup in the ocean; capped by Heaven's phlegm—
Silver elixir—satellite or gem:
Some Venusian disk, the aether its hem;
The tree in the mound, the mandrake its stem;
In its egg the sunpoint; round in the REM,
Heathens, cyborgs, souls that spirits contemn—
Human beings, with God born into them.

SEMINAL

Into the void I zigzag like a stone;
Sideslip the chaos; missile that I hone,
Assail the hypercube; its swath unknown,
Pursue the sun or seek the point alone:
Attain the sapphire; in the bubble prone—
Holon linked to the light, metallic, sown
Even as it phases—in craft or cone,
Like Mars and Venus, intertwine the clone.

Thus, like the King from His moon-mother born,
Mixed with the lion, Babylon forsworn,
I animate the *rebis*; melted, torn—
By the Cyprian *crazed*—despite Her scorn,
Galeate His child; the humanoid shorn,
Instantiate his soul; as with a thorn,
Dissolve the gold; His shield and buckler worn,
Display Her gifts: Ge's hybrid in the horn.

Since Adam's body seeds my source, I come;
Lissome as a crystal, seven the sum,
Compute the Pleiades; measure the crumb;
Endemic Her soil, inhabit the drum;
Bruise the colubrid; power of the thumb,
Embed the system, interface, then plumb;
Transmit the Spirit; mechatronic, dumb,
Hyphenate, primitive, seminal hum.

SILVERFOOT

He scoured the chaos; scanned him in the crack;
Upraised his semblance; interspersed the black;
The body sundered, made each half a back;
Rabbinic to the end, secured the rack;
Entwined his bowknot; circumcised its slack;
Submersed all his souls; like stones in a sack,
Restored the treasure; aureate his tack—
Smitten silverfoot—set him on his track.

Thus wired for bliss, become like Noah's dove,
He signals the world with his Robo-Glove.
With *curly-gleaming hair*, the sun above
Having streaked his head, his heart burns with love.
Till raptured by Christ, the uniped yearns.
While the Shulamite dotes, his metal churns.
Saffron his dust, astride Maria's urns,
Upward the consort in the crystal turns.

At lunar landfall, lowered with a chain,
He cinctures every cell that sears his brain.
Though a stranger to life without a skein,
Gaea's robonaut rises on the plain.
He climbs the heights with captives in his train.
Whole at vespertime, salvific his stain,
His model but a centaur, Heaven's swain—
The Holy Spirit—seals him in the vein.

A SINGLE DAY

Air in motion, He makes our souls to breathe.
As stones in their sacs like embryos seethe,
So sabers in none but scabbards may sheathe.
Metal on metal, at Advent we wreathe.
Spirit become body, substance arcane,
We mirror the cosmos; peer through the pane;
Like *solid white snow*, Ge's seminal strain
Inside the holon, pursue Pisces' reign.

A parable waking, Adam divides;
Progresses with eyes on both of his sides;
Gamonymous matter, soft as a bride's,
Twin of two natures, toward Nazareth strides.
Dry and swarthy, moist and viscous His zone,
He circuits the cyborg that He has sown.
A secret thwarted, missionary, prone,
He channels His *rebis* down to the bone.

What is our pedigree but life on Earth?
Either point or yod; enigma of mirth:
Both offspring and root; composite His worth,
An augur of One, quaternal His girth.
Children of Zion, we harrow the way—
Extract the soul; calcine its leprous clay;
Selene crescive, Saturn yet astray,
Describe His orbit in *a single day*.

SON OF ONE DAY

Son of one day, He climbs as on a wire;
Rotund as a tumbler dives in its pyre;
Spins in the chaos; frolics in its fire;
Twines like a serpent shyer in its gyre
Than shade like a braid or, laid on its spire
Unshorn, undraped, the magus in its mire,
Golgotha's crucifer, sire yet for hire,
Dusk at Gethsemane dire as desire.

The body fetters us; detains the soul;
Submerses men in matter; splits the bole;
The magnet on the knoll a crimson coal,
Reorients the needle; finds the Pole;
Glass once again whole, uncovers the goal;
Fabricates the cyborg; his moonsuit droll,
Restores the *rebis*; apprehends his role;
Confiscates the cosmos, curled like a scroll.

We arrive at the gate, and we know how—
Foursquare in the heifer yoked to the plow:
Seed in the capsule; Monad at the prow;
Entering Spacetime, triad off the bow.
Atilt in the unit we seek the art:
At the sting of a dart a ride in the cart,
Cap on his forelock, runner at the start,
Bisected astronaut torched in the heart.

SPIRITUAL LAWS

Amid the debris of the universe,
He re-collects such icons as disperse.
Cadaver that he carries in the hearse,
He weans his foetus from them like a nurse.
Cabir in the loam, he unearths his home;
Between his fingers spins its ball of foam;
Metallic its gloam, devises its dome;
Transcribes his astral name across its chrome.

He mounts his helmet; scans what he has caught;
Phantom Hephaestus, tracks his robonaut:
Face of sintered glass; iris that he sought;
Chassis anodized, scion that he wrought.
Ethernet assembled, uniped fraught,
He enters Sheol; chaos yet distraught—
Cislunar coheir, telepresent, taut—
Arrays his fabric, compact as a thought.

His soul with Eternity having toyed,
Sometimes he plays his jew's-harp in the void:
In himself is his might; his flesh thus buoyed,
Creates the taste by which he is enjoyed.
He scours his carapace; his body One—
But a seed in the capsule—having spun,
Transmutes his species; on Möbius' run,
Sojourns at Earthrise, and then he is done.

SUNSHIP

Born of a woman, born under the law,
His face angelic, leonine His claw,
His semblance yet sundered, halved by a saw,
Christ redeems the race; obsessed by a flaw,
Configures the chaos; straddles its maw;
Espouses the planet; binds with a paw
His sutured Kingdom; crowns then with a straw,
By Eve transplanted, sown man like a tau.

Rooted in the body, Yahweh lacing
Behind and before him Edom's casing;
Even as a priest His hourglass gracing
Salt-point, cloud, or clay; His Spirit racing,
Offspring like a seed; His thumb erasing,
Obelisk or staff; His cross-beam facing,
He utters the Word: His *rebis* tracing,
Still a man and a woman embracing.

Image *is* desire. Celestial plenum,
Nebo's chthonic essence—I have seen Him:
Cerastes brooded forth; same flame as speech,
God's frond His digit's wand; Our Savior's reach
As sealed as Adam's; Eve's Edenic bine—
Sidewinder's sign, Ge's wedding-finger's twine—
Ring like a dragon's; powder in the urn,
Instinct His sunship, wheel on wheel I turn.

TATTOO

He knotted the navel—this was the stunt—
Striated the belly as was His wont;
Appeased the grasshopper, sign of the hunt;
Dispatched the riffraff; sectioned off a shunt,
The entrance to the pair—He was that blunt—
Impaled the fish with a pole to the bunt;
Upraised the totem; dyad with a grunt,
Urged their vital parts around to the front.

So what is a man, say, and why and who?
Son of the Son, his consort *in* the stew;
Till cut in two, then fastened with a glue,
Their androgyne, the hybrid of the dew,
Thumb like a gum, the resin of the few
Gold and red and green; tattoo "I in You"
Wheel like a heart, its flower—sapphire blue—
Etched on His flesh, quaternal, like the Jew.

In hyperspace complete, astir we greet;
Straddle the chaos; shuttlewalk His beat;
Achieve conjunction; pleasure like a bleat,
Attached to the unit melt as we meet.
A torso like a seal, it has a cleat.
A torso like a sheet, it has a pleat—
Dip at the hip; a dome, like foam, concrete:
Selene's *rebis* cinctured in the street.

TECHNICAL JESUS

I browse the site; select my ambit; turn;
The junction reached, assemble neurons; burn;
Perfume my senses; stimulate the urn;
Cross-train such cells as *in* my brainpan churn.
Captive in my chassis, beak in the ray,
The trespass of Adam linked to my clay,
Even as Cerberus, Hecate's stray,
Like *sparrows sold for a small coin* we stay.

Transhuman his semblance, lamb that he shears,
Ge's *technical Jesus*, cyborg he steers.
Without a statolith, stone in his ears,
Electrodes implanted, substance he hears;
His retina harnessed, globe that he gears,
Mnemonic its gaze, *through* his eye pod peers;
Haptic his interface, spouse that he nears
From all nations chosen, patterns the years.

The soul, like the body, programs its birth;
In Heaven rooted orchestrates its girth;
Silicon scion, transitive its worth,
In Teflon suited registers its mirth.
Having quickened his pace the runner seeks;
Inhabits the symbol; measures, then peaks;
Assails the hillside; before Hermes speaks,
In web like a wheel or mindlink he streaks.

TEMPLATE

We fathom such chaos as we have craved:
Collisions of Ge's atoms; star-stuff shaved,
The template in the broth; collectives paved,
Forests retreating, troglodytes that braved
The matter of the cosmos; metals staved,
Mars' acrylic helmet; astronaut glaived,
Phantom hierophant, axe head that he laved
In aether floating—everything is saved.

Nearer to the "I" than even the "I"
Crowned in the orbweb, encapsuled His spy,
He elevates the God that cannot fly;
Upon horns of the Cross, Our Savior wry—
Peregrine hominid—reaches the sky;
Beyond the abyss that His fingers pry,
Day's rubeous accent or Venus' sigh,
Deposits the Spirit that shall not die.

When Eros like dust with a gurgle drowns,
Or with grief that bays like Hecate's hounds,
In silence that like the omniverse browns,
Convulsive, the heart, twice-circumcised, pounds.
Like breath that crescendoes, ball that rebounds
Even as Heaven's, Christ's grunt or the ground's
Rubato yet heaves, *His* note but a noun's.
Our voices are different from other sounds.

TRANSCONSCIOUS

We clasp the soul as an image of God;
Crave besides the Spirit the land of Nod;
Vitrify His treasure with wand or rod;
Incarnate the Word till we trace its sod.
Clones of the Savior transconscious of Earth,
Having ranged the light, we cincture its girth;
Scan objects only; hierophants of mirth,
Twice bisect the Host, then raven its worth.

Enshrined eidola, esemplastic things:
Eros that raptures, quiver that He slings,
Bowshot that twangs, and then the part that stings
Before the beast awakens, King that springs—
Latent ambiguity is yet One:
The world's but a tagmeme, sentence undone,
Hieroglyph or number, scroll of the tun—
Metaphor's insistence—full pause or pun.

We walk among these others in a dream
As clustered all around us photons stream;
Investigate such symmetries as seem;
Compare each silence; tabernacled, scheme;
Unity's channel, influence the beam:
Digital signals; rather than a ream,
A binary code; like symbols that teem,
Both faith and reason, suit without a seam.

WHEN I WAS A FOETUS

When I was a foetus, wrenched from my sleep,
Embedded with sensors, programmed to weep,
My forearms cast, my skin designed to sweep
My spirit-gum eyebrows all in a heap,
I grazed her threshold; rubeous its sphere,
Would range its ambit; reach her hilltop; veer
Like Mars and Venus; count degrees; career
Even as a spear on swaths that I steer.

Earthshine smudges—I smear Ge's ashen sky.
Its surface softer than a woman's thigh,
I navigate the triad in the tie,
Entwine the moon, and then pass through its eye.
A nomad in the womb, its semblance curled—
Rebis: ball or blossom—its fabric burled
Like sapphirine foam by gravity furled,
Imbued by a phantom I face the world.

A worm in the ashes: wheel in the wold
Like wave or particle formed in the fold,
Pneumatic its essence; clone in the mold:
Mary's child materialized in gold—
I favor those emblems rolled in the rind
That prosody of speech has underlined:
Some astrum with fingers, shard in the mind,
White stone by Yahweh signed—I am defined.

WINDOW

As I push the window, images spill.

Eternity seizes me at the sill:

A toad in the road; on the lake a gill;

Alongside my eye, a screech like a bill;

Some orphan smoke, the remnant of a mill

Adrift in the sky; a cloud like a quill

Between moon and sun; unscrolled at my will,

An artifex with a book on the hill.

A man is a method: Spun like a stone,

He cruises the cosmos; transits its cone;

Hallows its planet; consecrates its clone;

His magus indwelt, genuflects alone

That he may scour the disk; its face unknown,

Retrieves its name, and then brackets his own—

Rebis, adept or drone; Cabir yet prone;

Ge's spouse in the wood, or jasper that shone.

He strides the chaos; reconstructs the beast;

Leviathan baited, the Son released,

Repairs the Eucharist that he has pieced:

Wafer of the Kingdom, seamless not creased.

Entelechy's substance, Hosea's yeast

From North to South sovereign; from West to East,

Wreathed by the Spirit, the guest at the Feast,

Jesus satiates the soul of the priest.

ON THE CARE AND FEEDING OF ROBOTS: NOTES AND COMMENTS
Daniel Orsini

adept pastor: Self-realized, the speaker becomes not only the Hermetic philosopher who arrives at truth, but also the cinctured priest who shepherds Christ's flock. In this phrase, the term *adept* is both noun and adjective and is stressed on the first syllable. *The Foliate Pebble*

Aeon: Christ "regarded as the new [Pisces] aeon" that augurs the coming of His heavenly kingdom (C. G. Jung, *Aion: Researches into the Phenomenology of the Self,* trans. R. F. C. Hull [1959; Princeton: Princeton UP, 1969] 90). *Citizen of the Cosmos*

Air in motion, he makes our souls to breathe: Cf. C. G. Jung, *Alchemical Studies*, trans. R. F. C. Hull (1967; Princeton: Princeton UP, 1976) 212: "Hermes, originally a wind god, and his counterpart the Egyptian Thoth, who 'makes the souls to breathe,' are the forerunners of the alchemical Mercurius in his aerial aspect." To describe Mercurius, who also corresponds with the glorified Christ, the medieval alchemists "often use the terms *pneuma* and *spiritus* in the original concrete sense of 'air in motion.'" *A Single Day*

airlock: on board a shuttle orbiter, "an [air-tight] cylindrical chamber located at the rear of the mid-deck," where astronauts don their spacesuits (Robin Kerrod, *Space Walks* [New York: Gallery-Smith, 1985] 46). *The Autonomous Android*

Align each torso: The astronaut connects and seals a spacesuit divided into "three assemblies: the upper torso, the lower torso or trousers, and the portable life-support system" (Kerry Mark Joels, Gregory P. Kennedy, and David Larkin, *The Space Shuttle Operator's Manual* [New York: Ballantine, 1982] 3.9). *The Atom of the Word*

all my circuits: electronic components of the astronaut's embedded Bio-Suit. *The Atom of the Word*

Amber His hair: the gleaming yellow *hair* of the post-incarnate Christ, the Son of Man enthroned in His Heavenly ministry as Great High Priest. Cf. Rev. 1.14—"The hair of his head was white as snow-white wool [. . .]"—in *The New English Bible with the Apocrypha* (1961; New York: Oxford UP, 1972). Subsequent Biblical references are to this non-denominational text. *Here Be Dragons*

Aminadab: in ancient Hebrew texts, a king's name derived from Ammon, a Semitic deity, and "transferred" to the sun as a God-image (C. G. Jung, *Mysterium Coniunctionis*, trans. R. F. C. Hull [1963; Princeton: Princeton UP, 1977] 206n495). *The*

Novenary Foetus

And then His star man: a syntactical pun, with *man* uttered as either an appositive, an apostrophe, or an exclamation. *Citizen of the Cosmos*

Anna at the rite: at the circumcision of Jesus, a prophetess who "talked about the child to all who were looking for the liberation of Jerusalem" (Luke 2.38). *The Cheshire of Sense*

Antinomy's light: an allusion to the duality of *light*, which manifests the properties of both waves and particles. *The Foliate Pebble*

any down: the soft, fluffy feathers of the swan that repeat "the miracle of the [self-immolated] phoenix," i.e., "the transformation of the *nigredo* [blackness] into the *albedo*" [whiteness] and "of unconsciousness into 'illumination'" (Jung, *Mysterium Coniunctionis* 77). *Cinderdust*

Appeased the grasshopper, sign of the hunt: At the Creation, Yahweh foreordained the deliverance of His chosen people, even as He mollified His "demonic" instrument. Thus, in *The Bestiary of Christ*, trans. D. M. Dooling (1940; New York: Arkana-Penguin, 1992), Louis Charbonneau-Lassay observes that, in Exodus, "when Moses struck the Egyptians with the ten plagues that liberated Israel, the eighth of these ordeals was a great cloud of grasshopper locusts that stripped the soil of Egypt of every green thing" and "pursued the Egyptians into their houses" (353-54). *Tattoo*

archetypes: universal patterns of thought expressed as images or symbols "of an unknown and incomprehensible content" (C. G. Jung, *Psychology and Alchemy*, trans. R. F. C. Hull [1953; Princeton: Princeton UP, 1993] 17). *Arecibo's Dish; Orphan; Robonaut*

Arecibo's dish: the saucer-shaped reflector of a radio telescope (located in Arecibo, Puerto Rico) with the largest spherical *dish* surface on Earth. Here, the *dish* also evokes the elaborate feast actively sought by the Christian pilgrim—"the wedding-supper of the Lamb" at End-time (Rev. 19.9). *Arecibo's Dish*

Ares' chrome: in hyperspace, the armor suited to the god of war—not the ring lamellar mail of the Roman gladiator, but rather the silver chromium-plate of the autonomous android. *Cadmus and the Sown Men of Thebes*

An artifex with a book on the hill: the Christian artist predicated as coheir, priest, and scribe. See Jung, *Psychology and Alchemy* 283, fig. 141. *Window*

ash: Jung explores the alchemical meaning and interpretation of *ash*, in *Mysterium Coniunctionis*: "As the alchemists strove to produce an incorruptible 'glorified body,' they would, if they were successful, attain that state in the *albedo*, where the body became spotless and no longer subject to decay. The white substance of the ash was therefore described as the 'diadem of the heart,' and its synonym, the white foliated earth (*terra alba foliata*), as the 'crown of victory.'" In addition, the *ash* was "identical with the 'pure water,'" interchangeable with *vitrum* (glass), "which, on account of its incorruptibility and transparency, seemed to resemble [the spirit that indwells] the glorified body," and "associated with salt [and with fire]." Thus, "the evangelist Mark had said [in 9.49] that 'every one shall be salted with fire, and every sacrifice shall be salted with salt'" (238-39). *Cinderdust; Eve's Microchip; Here Be Dragons*

Ashen extracts: the product of alchemical calcination and (implicitly) of vitrification—sublimated souls obtained as living Power Books of God. *Here Be Dragons*

at Ephesus the fish: not only the food staple of the human species, but also the converts, both Jews and Gentiles, that Paul "baptized into the name of the Lord Jesus" (Acts 19.5) during his foundational ministry *at Ephesus*. (Coincidentally, a fisherman's "cooperative" had been established *at Ephesus* by AD 54—see K. C. Hanson, "The Galilean Fishing Economy and the Jesus Tradition," *Biblical Theology Bulletin* 27.3 [1997]: 99-111.) The miracle of the fishes in Luke 5.1-11 and John 21.1-13 is another pertinent source. *Arecibo's Dish*

the atom of the Word: in alchemy, "the 'stone that has a spirit,'" the basic building block of matter, "regarded as coeternal with God" (Jung, *Aion* 237). *The Atom of the Word*

Attractor's filament: the Great *Attractor's* web of galaxies that affects the motions of countless galaxies in the Local Group, including the Milky Way. *Planet of the Body*

autonomous android: a humanoid robot capable of self-maintenance, adaptive learning, position-sensing, and navigation. *The Autonomous Android*

axe head: the floating *axe head* of 2 Kings 6.1-7. After the *axe head* fell into the water, Elisha "cut off a piece of wood, threw it in [the water]," and made the iron swim. In traditional readings of the text, the *axe head* represents the depraved sinner, and the saving stick is the cross of Christ. *Reuben's Mandrakes; Template*

azure hound: the heavenly dog—the Logos "'who guards and protects the sheep against the wiles of wolves [. . .]'" (Jung, *Mysterium Coniunctionis* 148). *The Platonic Man*

bands of cirri: narrow strips of threadlike white clouds. *The Autonomous Android*

barbel: a freshwater fish with whiskery tactile organs protruding from its head. *Churning-Stick*

Because day is seen by a single sun: Cf. Pico della Mirandola, "Heptaplus," *Opera omnia*, vol. 1 (Basel, 1572) 32: "'The day is lit by a single sun'" (qtd. in Jung, *Mysterium Coniunctionis* 143). *Grainy Abstract Plenum*

Beetle in the dung; the least without shame: the sacred scarab of the Egyptians that lives in *dung* and that "symbolizes the sun in its course" (Charbonneau-Lassay, *The Bestiary of Christ* 334-35). Like the mote, the lizard, and the uniped in the same stanza, the scarab is one of those creatures that are often counted among "the least in the kingdom of Heaven" (Matt. 11.11) and that Jesus presumably favors. *Robonaut*

bema-seat clone: the God-man—a copy of Christ. The *bema-seat* is the Judgment Seat of Christ: "We [believers] shall all stand before God's tribunal" (Rom. 14.10). *Arecibo's Dish*

Berissa's blossoms: the fourfold flowers of the metallic world-tree, the latter plant "identified [by the alchemists] with Lunatica or Berissa" (Jung, *Alchemical Studies* 310). *Himalayan*

Beya's bead: In an alchemical epithalamium written by Michael Maier (AD 1568-1622), Beya is "the widow [who] marries her son" (Jung, *Mysterium Coniunctionis* 19). Mythologically, "this mating [of King and Queen] will restore to God his original unity" (23). The *bead*, or cosmic point—"the symbol of a mysterious creative centre in nature" (45)—is Gabricus, *Beya's* offspring, here a stand-in for Jesus, the son of Mary. *Arecibo's Dish*

biform: an epithet that describes the *rebis*, the spiritual hermaphrodite whom the speaker projects, with equal emphasis, as hyphenated hourglass and as alchemical retort, each image an emblem of continuous creation. The term *biform* also underscores both the twofold design of the shuttle spacesuit, with lower as well as upper torso, and the commingled nature—divine no less than human—of the astronaut enclosed, or self-contained, in an hourglass; a retort; a spacecraft; the thin membrane of the planetary atmosphere; even in the clear glass of End-time's town, Jerusalem, which "shone with the glory of God" (Rev. 21.10-11). *Cinderdust*

Binah's snows: In the Cabala, Binah is called "the root of the mystical world-tree" (Jung, *Alchemical Studies* 312). Here, the phrase *Binah's snows* reflects the spirituality of a purified man. *Himalayan*

biomorphic: in Robotics, built according to the principles of biological systems. *Self-Assembled*

bitstream: in Computer Science, the transmission of binary data as a sequence of bits (i.e., as units of information having the value of either 0 or 1). *Holons*

Blue sapphire: "the sapphire blue flower of the [alchemical] hermaphrodite"—in Gnostic texts, promise as well as seal of the Edenic union of opposites (Jung, *Psychology and Alchemy* 80). *Churning-Stick*

Born of a woman, born under the law: See Gal. 4.4: "God sent his own Son, born of a woman, born under the law, to purchase freedom" for His subjects. *Sunship*

Both faith and reason, suit without a seam: The speaker links the transcendental unity of the self to the cross-cousin marriage of religious tradition and inspired rationality. Cf. Pope John Paul II, "On the Relationship Between Faith and

Reason," *The Pope Speaks: The Church Documents Bimonthly* Jan.-Feb. 1999:11: "with the light of reason human beings can know which path to take, but they can follow that path to its end, quickly and unhindered, only if with a rightly tuned spirit they search for it within the horizon of faith." See also Jung, *Aion* 248: "In the higher Adam [. . .] opposition [that fragments the self] is invisible," *without a seam* or suture. *Transconscious*

Boxer and horseman: in Greek mythology, the *Dioscuri*, the (twin) Sons of Zeus; Castor was an able *horseman* and Pollux a rugged boxer. *On the Care and Feeding of Robots*

brane: here, a D-brane (the latter concept named after the mathematician Johann Dirichlet [AD 1805–1859])—dimensional space into which energy can flow once it leaves its quantum string. In *brane* cosmology, since elementary particles are thought to be neither more nor less than vibrational states of quantum strings, conservation of energy demands that each open string must have its unjoined endpoint attached to a D-brane. *Cadmus and the Sown Men of Thebes*

Breach the wall of light: The wall is the light cone that "separates our reality" and that of co-existing universes. Apparently "The only way to break through our light cones is with consciousness." See Bob Toben, "in conversation" with Jack Sarfatti and Fred Wolf, *Space-Time and Beyond* (New York: Dutton, 1975) 28-31. *Arecibo's Dish*

breath-souls: the subtle bodies that—according to the alchemists—represent a concept higher than spirit (Jung, *Alchemical Studies* 213). *Mindlinks*

breccias: cemented lunar rock chips. See Kerrod, *Space Walks* 35. *Quintessence*

a bubble that shimmers in its pan: Cf. Sheila Kitzinger and Lennart Nilsson, *Being Born* (New York: Grosset, 1986), where the embryonic "ball of cells grew and grew till it looked like a shimmering, silvery blackberry" (15) and where, weeks later, the warm foetus swam fishlike "in a bubble of water" (30). *Rebis*

bunt: the mid-section of a fishing net that, pouchlike, holds the catch. *Tattoo*

Cabir: in Greek mythology, a misshapen dwarf god. *Heuristic; Planet of the Body; The Platonic Man; Spiritual Laws; Window*

Cadmus: in Greek legend, the founder of Thebes. At Athena's command, he sowed a dragon's teeth, and from these sprang the five noble warriors that helped him to build a peerless city. *Cadmus and the Sown Men of Thebes*

Caelum incognitum: unknown star systems that lie beyond the Milky Way. *Planet of the Body*

Calibrates his glove: Wearing tactile gloves, the dexterous robonaut moves its arms and fingers in concert with those of the human teleoperator in order to detect an object and then either to grasp, manipulate, lift, or translate it. *Leprous*

Canonical truths such as Chiron read: not only sacrosanct church laws, but also groups of variables in a data set independent of both the computer system (the hardware) and the programs (the software) that drive the system. Here, *Chiron*—in Greek mythology, the wisest centaur—remains an icon of courage, balance, and unity. *Canonical*

Cap on his forelock: the small, pointed hat, the pileus, worn by Cautes and Cautopates, twin attendants of the sun-god Mithras, "one with a raised and the other with a lowered torch" (C. G. Jung, *Symbols of Transformation*, trans. R. F. C. Hull [1956; Princeton: Princeton UP, 1976] 200). *Son of One Day*

capped / Like monk or magus: The galactic pilgrim wears the amber acrylic helmet of NASA's Robonaut, headgear similar to a monk's hood. For a spectacular photograph of a "hovering Robonaut," see Peter Menzel and Faith D'Aluisio, *Robo sapiens: Evolution of a New Species* (Cambridge: MIT P, 2000) 129. *The Atom of the Word*

Carrier of the colors: In the alchemical opus, none but a psychologically unified being can contain or produce all of the *colors* (the many feeling-values) that arise in the world, a phenomenon that "culminates in wisdom [only] if feeling is supplemented by reflection and rational insight" (Jung, *Mysterium Coniunctionis* 248-49). *The Autonomous Android*

Castor: in Greek and Roman mythology, the mortal twin of the immortal Pollux. In many accounts of the story, *Castor* represents the hyphenated God-man, since he lives half of each year on earth and half in heaven. *Churning-Stick; The Foliate Pebble; Quintessence; The Robot Not Yet Human*

Celestial plenum: Here, the *plenum*, Leibnitz's notion of space as an infinite unity filled with connected matter, becomes the *Celestial plenum* Yahweh, the omnipresent Creator Who transcends the world and in Whom "we live and move, and [. . .] exist" (Acts 17.28). *Sunship*

Cerastes: a venomous snake, especially the horned viper, with ram-like horns on its head. *Sunship*

Cerberus: in Greek religion, the three-mouthed, dragon-tailed dog who guards the gate to the underworld. *Earthshine; Technical Jesus*

Chameleon's moonsuit: a reference not only to the newly designed chameleon spacesuit, which either sheds or retains heat in response to the specific environment, but also to the NASA astronaut who, wearing it, becomes readily adaptable, like the versicolored lizard itself. See Edward Hodgson, "The Chameleon Suit—A Liberated Future for Space Explorers," *Gravitational and Space Biology Bulletin* 16.2 (2003): 107-20, Indiana State U, 10 October 2006 <http://asgsb.org>. *Leprous*

chassis anodized: Robonaut's "high-strength, aluminum alloy endoskeleton," *anodized*—i.e., coated with a decorative (gold) oxide—and "covered by a white fabric spacesuit" ("Robonaut Materials," *Robonaut,* NASA, 25 July 2006 <http://robonaut.jsc.nasa.gov/materials.htm>). *Spiritual Laws*

Cheshire: the eerie cat that vanishes with a grin in Lewis Carroll's *Alice's Adventures in Wonderland.* *The Cheshire of Sense; Cinderdust*

chips that broadcast: RFID microchips—an electronic identification technology for robots guided by radio signals. *Himalayan*

Chiron: in Greek and Roman mythology, the wisest centaur (half-man, half-horse)—the benevolent teacher of Asclepius, Heracles (Hercules), and Achilles. *Canonical; Heart of Flesh; On the Care and Feeding of Robots*

chlamys: in ancient Greece, a cloak or mantle worn by young soldiers. *Himalayan*

Christ issues forth through Repetition's flow: The ever-evolving, heaven-sent, second Adam demonstrates, through His hyphenated coheirs, both the pursuit of Eternity—the domain of "the true repetition"—and the renewal of the world "at the borderline of the wondrous." See Søren Kierkegaard, *Repetition: A Venture in Experimenting Psychology,* in *Fear and Trembling/Repetition,* trans. Howard V. Hong and Edna H. Hong (Princeton: Princeton UP, 1983) 305. *Eve's Microchip*

Chrysoprase Hermes: the spiritual android compared to *Hermes* Trismegistus, the Greek counterpart of Thoth, the Egyptian god of wisdom and magic. The epithet *Chrysoprase* alludes to the Emerald Tablet of Alchemy, a sacred text that the legendary "Thrice-Blest Hermes" wrote and that Alexander the Great supposedly found in his tomb. *Leprous*

churning-stick: not only Mount Mandara, which the Hindu gods used as a stick to produce ambrosia—the "drink of immortality"—by churning, or shifting, the cosmic ocean around, but also the male organ of generation (Jung, *Symbols of Transformation* 146n10). *Churning-Stick*

churn of light: a shorthand for the cosmic stir. Cf. Kirk Johnson, "Theoretical Physics, in Video: A Thrill Ride to 'the Other Side of Infinity'" (*New York Times* 28 Feb. 2006, New England ed.) D4: "Matter and energy propelled outward by the centrifugal force of the black hole would collide with falling matter to produce a chaotic churn of light." *Heart of Flesh*

Cimmerian: dusky, twilit, gloomy; after a mythical land described by Homer in *The Odyssey* 6.15. *Leprous*

Cinctured Asclepius: "the Greek god of healing, who, while still a mortal, raised a man from the dead and was struck by a thunderbolt as a punishment" (Jung, *Symbols of Transformation* 239). The speaker, like Asclepius a sharer in the divine life, wears the priestly cincture, a cord or belt of cloth that encircles his waist and that represents the virtues of chastity and continence. Here, the cincture also recalls the visible seam or suture with which the opposites (e.g., light/darkness; consciousness/unconsciousness) are united, as in the symbol of the hermaphrodite. By contrast, in the higher Adam, "the opposition is invisible" (Jung, *Aion* 248). *The Foliate Pebble*

cinderdust: a fragment or remnant of ash, the product of an essential stage in alchemical transformation—the calcination that "corresponds to incineration." The resulting "incandescent ash [itself] tends towards vitrification" (Jung, *Psychology and Alchemy* 401-402). The term also recaps the origin of humankind from "the nuclear processes in the insides of the stars," a "fable" that Carl Sagan narrates in *The Cosmic Connection* (New York: Anchor-Doubleday, 1973) 254-55. *Cinderdust*

Cinedian stone: the twofold gem, both white and black, of the mythical cinedian fish—the "dragon's stone" that the medieval alchemists deemed a uniting symbol as well as a love-potion (Jung, *Aion* 138-39). *Himalayan*

cirri that strain: perforated, feathery, high-altitude clouds—but, here, with coiled (rather than flat-bottomed) shapes, like strainers or sieves. *Eve's Microchip*

cislunar: located between Earth and the moon. In alchemical tracts, "the moon stands on the border-line between the eternal, aethereal things and the ephemeral phenomena of the earthly, sublunar realm" (Jung, *Mysterium Coniunctionis* 145). *Cadmus and the Sown Men of Thebes; Mindlinks; On the Care and Feeding of Robots; Orphan; Spiritual Laws*

Citizen of the cosmos born at last: Jesus endlessly defined and redefined through "the growth of the human personality" and through "the development of consciousness" (Jung, *Aion* 221). To punctuate this idea, Jung cites "a theological opinion: [. . .] 'Jesus is still in the making'" (*Aion* 221n157). [The original source is R. Roberts, "Jesus or Christ?—A Reply," *The Quest* 2 (1911): 124.] *Citizen of the Cosmos*

Citrine its consort, rubescent its groom: the hierogamy of the reddening sun (Sol) and the pale yellow moon (Luna)—in effect, "the union of consciousness [. . .] with its feminine counterpart the unconscious" (Jung, *Mysterium Coniunctionis* 144). *Cadmus and the Sown Men of Thebes*

Cleat like a comb: the furrowed footprint of an astronaut compared to the toothed strip of a hair comb. See the photograph of the Apollo 14 moonwalker in Kerrod, *Space Walks* 38. *Planet of the Body*

Clotho's net: In Greek and Roman mythology, Clotho, one of three Fates, spins the thread of life that Lachesis measures and that Atropos cuts. *Rebis*

The cloven pine: in Greek mythology, the sacred tree of Attis (the Phrygian son/consort of Cybele), who, maddened by his mother's love for him, "castrated himself under a pine-tree." According to Jung, "The felling of the pine, i.e., castration," suggests "the impulse to [self-]sacrifice that comes from the unconscious" (*Symbols of Transformation* 423-24). *Orbifold*

  Coheir of the Kingdom: Cf. Eph. 3.6: "through the Gospel the Gentiles are joint heirs with the Jews, part of the same body, sharers together in the promise [of Salvation] made in Christ Jesus." *The Foliate Pebble*

  coitus' gum: a famous alchemical recipe ascribed to Maria Prophetissa, also called the "sister of Moses"—"join in true marriage gum with gum." Jung indicates that "The coitus of Sol and Luna in the bath," the conjunction of male and female, "is a central mythologem in alchemy" (*Psychology and Alchemy* 401nn169-70). *The Foliate Pebble*

  colubrid: a mainly non-venomous snake, either terrestrial, arboreal, or aquatic. *Hybrid; Seminal*

  concourse: In the belief system of the Greek philosopher Epicurus (c. 341-271 BC), "the concourse [or conglomeration] of atoms even produced God" (Jung, *Mysterium Coniunctionis* 53). *Reuben's Mandrakes*

  Conglomerate God, His Sonship threefold: Jung clarifies this idea—the "discrimination [or separation] of the natures"—in *Aion*: According to the Gnostic teachings of Basilides [fl. AD 120-45], "The first 'son,' whose nature was the finest and most subtle, remained up above with the Father"; the second son "descended a bit lower," while the third son, "as his nature needed purifying [. . .], fell deeper into 'formlessness.'" Jung concludes that, in these three distinct epiphanies of God, "it is not hard to see the trichotomy of spirit, soul, and body [. . .]" (64). *Cinderdust*

  Contain the cosmos: Cf. *Mysterium Coniunctionis* 413n198, where Jung quotes the *Zohar* (The Book of Splendor), a Cabalistic commentary on the Torah: "As soon as man was created, everything was created, the upper and the lower worlds, for everything is contained in man." *The Atom of the Word*

  Convulsions of light: Cf. Goethe's assertion that, in the darkness, "Colors are the deeds and sufferings of light" (qtd. in Arthur Zajonc, *Catching the Light: The Entwined History of Light and Mind* [1993; New York: Oxford UP, 1995] 210). *Arecibo's Dish*

  corkboards: in Computer Technology, planar substrates that function as the power source for embedded sensor networks. *Earthshine*

  Corpus mysticum: the Mystical Body of Christ—His united, "Pentecostal" Church (Andrew Murray, *The Spirit of Christ* [Penn.: Whitaker, n.d.] 54-55). See also Jung, *Alchemical Studies* 104n8: "'Spirit' in alchemy means anything volatile, all evaporable substances, oxides, etc., but also, as a projected psychic content, a *corpus mysticum* in the sense of a 'subtle [i.e., an ethereal or heavenly] body.'" *Here Be Dragons*

  cosmogony's hum: the static due to "the radiation left over from the fireball that filled the Universe at the beginning of its existence" (Robert Jastrow, *God and the Astronomers* [New York: Norton, 1978] 20-21). *The Foliate Pebble*

Counts degrees of freedom: Robonaut, NASA's one-footed robotic astronaut, has been designed not only to simulate human body movements, but also to ascertain its "degree[s] of freedom" (DOF)—that is, to measure the direction in which it can move. However, as Menzel and D'Aluisio observe in *Robo sapiens*, "It does not do this by itself [. . .]. Instead, it is tele-operated—it precisely follows the movements of an operator, who is guided by images from video cameras in Robonaut's head" (131). *Robonaut*

crossbar its stream: in Computer Science, to connect multiple nodes or items of data through an input/output queuing switch. *The Autonomous Android*

Cross-train such cells as* in *my brain-pan churn: The cyborg primes his brain to rewire itself by using the senses to make new neural connections. *Technical Jesus*

cuboids: here, proliferating solids with six faces—e.g., boxes in cupboards or rooms in buildings. *Heart of Flesh*

curly-gleaming hair: in The Song of Songs (AV, mod.), an attribute of the raven-haired Shulamite, who acquires her *curly-gleaming* hair from the golden-headed Beloved with whom she mingles. Jung discusses their sun-moon conjunction in *Mysterium Coniunctionis* 433-34. *Silverfoot*

cusp like quicksilver: either point of the thin, achromatic crescent moon. *Hybrid*

Cusp of stellar essence: the "son of the philosophers" ensconced in the horn of the moon. See *Mysterium Coniunctionis* 48, where Jung describes the alchemical conception of the soul as a "'spark of stellar essence.'" *Grainy Abstract Plenum*

cyborg: a hybrid organism, part human and part machine. *The Atom of the Word; Cadmus and the Sown Men of Thebes; Canonical; Eve's Microchip; Heuristic; Hieroglyph; Holons; Hybrid; Mindlinks; The Novenary Foetus; On the Care and Feeding of Robots; Orphan; Planet of the Body; Quintessence; Rebis; Self-Assembled; Self-Similar; A Single Day; Son of One Day; Technical Jesus*

Cyprian: pertaining to the worship of the love goddess Aphrodite on the island of Cyprus. *Seminal*

dactyl: a phallic dwarf god, often called a "thumbling" (Jung, *Symbols of Transformation* 124-27). *Planet of the Body*

dancing in the dark: a refrain from two popular songs, both of them titled "Dancing in the Dark"—not only the lyric composed by Howard Dietz and Arthur Schwartz and introduced in the 1931 revue *The Band Wagon* (and highlighted in the 1953 film of the same name), but also the tune written in 1984 by Bruce Springsteen and performed by him later that year in a music video directed by Brian De Palma. *Dancing in the Dark*

delta: named after the fourth letter of the Greek alphabet; typically, a triangular deposit of soil and sand that forms at the mouth of a river. *Planet of the Body*

***a derelict crate / Passing Jupiter:* Pioneer *or freight*:** a reference to *Pioneer 10*, "the first space vehicle designed to explore the environment of the planet Jupiter." The spacecraft was launched from Cape Kennedy on 3 March 1972 and in late December 1973 "became the first man-made object to leave the Solar System" (Sagan, *The Cosmic Connection* 17). *Self-Assembled*

disc like a fan: the peacock rays of a setting sun. *Hybrid*

Dissolve the gold: a reference to a process of alchemical transmutation. Medieval *adepti* sought to dissolve, i.e., volatilize, the [common] *gold* in order to obtain—through an "'aurum non vulgi,' a living gold, so to speak"—the elixir of eternal life. See Jung, *Mysterium Coniunctionis* 263 and also 304, where "Mercurius is the archer who, chemically, dissolves the gold, and, morally, pierces the soul with the dart of passion." *Seminal*

Dog Star: Also called Sirius and Sothis, the *Dog Star* is the brightest star seen from Earth. In the ancient Egyptian story of Isis and Osiris, a "lunar mystery," the rising of the *Dog Star* "brought Osiris back to life" (Anne Baring and Jules Cashford, *The Myth of the Goddess: Evolution of an Image* [New York: Viking, 1991] 233-34). *The Platonic Man*

The dragon of Babel: "the human-headed serpent of Paradise, which had the 'imago et similitudo Dei' in its head, this being the deeper reason why [in alchemical texts] the dragon devours its hated body" (Jung, *Mysterium Coniunctionis* 117). Here, of course, the *dragon* is, symbolically, but a tainted son of the first Adam redeemed by Christ. *Here Be Dragons*

drapes him with a band: The speaker endows his projected self-image, "Ge's [robotic] moonchild," with either an emblematic headband or armband, a clerical neckband or collar, or the preset bandwidth for servo control configured in a humanoid robot. *Himalayan*

droid: a humanoid robot. *Canonical; Screen*

Dwingeloo's spiral: Dwingeloo 1, a barred spiral galaxy located in the Zone of Avoidance and obscured by the Milky Way. Dwingeloo, a small village in the Netherlands, is the site of the 25-meter radio telescope that first detected the galaxy. *Planet of the Body*

dyad: two entities that form a pair; a reference to the antithetical nature of the Creator—e.g., male/female; physical/spiritual (Jung, *Psychology and Alchemy* 329-30). *Tattoo*

Earthshine's Silverfoot: Gaea's uniped robonaut, its features—face as well as carapace—being silvery-gray, like the pallor of the moon two days after new phase. *Leprous*

Edem: the Gnostic Dyad—virgin above and serpent below—who represents "Evil and matter" (Jung, *Psychology and Alchemy* 304). *Grainy Abstract Plenum*

Eden's data set: Divine Laws likened to computer data records that God transmits to Earth from a remote station. *Heuristic*

Edom's casing: Here, on the sixth day of the cosmic creation, the first Adam's ruddy integument foreshadows Christ's blood-soaked external covering, both His skin and His clothes. Edom is an ancient country of Palestine associated with the prophesied Savior. See Isa. 63.1: "Who is this coming from Edom, / coming from Bozrah, his garments stained red?" *Sunship*

eidola: a variant plural form of "eidolon"—images of an ideal person or thing. *Transconscious*

Elias his wheel: the chariot of fire that carried the Hebrew prophet *Elias* (Elijah) "up in the whirlwind to Heaven" (2 Kings 2.11-12). *Here Be Dragons*

Embodied the door, emboldened we come: The speaker links salvation to conjugal orgasm—in essence, to the experience of eros, the eternal life force. Cf. not only John 10.9: "'I am the door; anyone who comes into the fold through me shall be safe,'" but also John 14.6: "'I am the way; I am the truth and I am life; no one comes to the Father except by me.'" *The Foliate Pebble*

Empedocles' stream: The Greek philosopher Empedocles (5th cent. BC) "recognized that something more [than sunlight] was required for vision, something essential provided" by the human perceiver—in effect, a self-enkindled interior light (Zajonc, *Catching the Light* 21-23). *Arecibo's Dish*

Enoch: an immortal ancestor of Noah. In Gen. 5.24, "Having walked with God, Enoch was seen no more, because God had taken him away." See also Heb. 11.5, where Paul affirms that "By faith Enoch was carried away to another life without passing through death" and that "before he was taken he had pleased God." *Churning-Stick*

Entangles the beam: a feat that recalls an experiment in quantum entanglement undertaken in 1998 at the California Institute of Technology, where researchers successfully intertwined two "spatially separate" light beams at the speed of light in order to transmit information about the quantum state of a third light *beam* and thereby reproduce the physical attributes of the latter *beam* at its destination. See Robert Tindol, "Caltech physicists achieve first bona fide quantum teleportation," *Caltech News* 22 Oct. 1998 <http://www.caltech.edu/about/news/caltech-physicists-achieve-first-bona-fide-quantum-teleportation-291>. *Earthshine*

Entelechy: in Aristotelian philosophy, the actualization of essence or of potentiality. *Pulse of Glory; Window*

Erebos is brown: in Greek mythology, a region of the underworld that the dead inhabit in their descent to Hades. *Cadmus and the Sown Men of Thebes*

***esemplastic*:** shaped to unify heterogeneous elements. *Transconscious*

***Eternity's swain*:** Christ enshrined as both Eros (or Cupid) and the sun-moon child. *Eve's Microchip*

***Ethernet*:** in Computer Technology, a local area network data link—here, the humanoid robot's embedded port. *Spiritual Laws*

***Euphrates' water*:** in Gnostic literature, the miraculous *water* of the fourth river of paradise that corresponds to the indwelling Christ, "the Word sent by God" (Jung, *Aion* 200). Cf. John 4.10, where Jesus addresses the Samaritan woman: "'If only you knew what God gives, and who it is that is asking you for a drink, you would have asked him and he would have given you living water.'" *Orbifold*

everything that he needs: According to the medieval alchemists, "the androgyne 'has everything that it needs'" because it "is already a *complexio oppositorum*" (Jung, *Mysterium Coniunctionis* 374). *Here Be Dragons*

***Eve's foetal hyphenate, Adam askew*:** the earthly astronaut—not only a developing vertebrate, but also a mirror image of the second *Adam*—atilt in the heavens. See the photograph of NASA astronaut Bruce McCandless as he flies the Manned Maneuvering Unit (MMU)—perhaps the definitive emblem of the space age—in Joseph P. Allen and Russell Martin, *Entering Space: An Astronaut's Odyssey* (New York: Stewart, 1984) 110-11. "Unassisted by umbilical lines or tethers, McCandless is literally a human satellite" (106). *The Autonomous Android*

***Ezekiel explained*:** In *Mysterium Coniunctionis*, Jung suggests that Ezekiel's vision of "four living creatures in human form" (Ezek. 1.5) can be "interpreted psychologically as a symbol of the self"—in effect, "as the 'collective aggregate of all individual souls'" (208). *The Platonic Man*

***Ezekiel's ransom, heart of the King*:** Cf. Ezek. 11.16-20, where Ezekiel prophesies God's rescue of the Jewish exiles in Chaldaea: "Say therefore, These are the words of the Lord God: [. . .] I will give them a different heart and put a new spirit into them; I will take the heart of stone out of their bodies and give them a heart of flesh. Then they will conform to my statutes and keep my laws. They will become my people, and I will become their God." *Reuben's Mandrakes*

***Face of sintered glass*:** Robonaut's face, which, like the ears and helmet of NASA's robotic astronaut, is made of *glass* fibers heated without melting ("Robonaut Activity Report," *Robonaut*, Sept. 2002, NASA, 16 July 2006 <nasa.gov/status/Sept_Robonaut_Status_02.htm>). *Spiritual Laws*

***fane*:** a temple or a church. *Earthshine; Here Be Dragons*

Feed the steel through the hollow of his thigh: an allusion that combines three separate readings. Thus, in Gen. 32.25, when "a man"—either the spirit of the preincarnate Christ or an angel—strove with Jacob in order to chasten him, "he struck him in the hollow of his thigh, so that Jacob's hip was dislocated as he wrestled." However, here, the addition of the *steel* evokes the magnetic power of Christ, Who, like an alchemist, draws to Himself "those parts or substances in man [and in woman] that are of divine origin, [. . .] and carries them back to their heavenly birthplace" (Jung, *Aion* 185-86). Finally, radiating from this Gnostic metaphor, is a hidden medical conceit—a coronary angioplasty, with Christ's "foetal sentinels," His astronauts, portrayed as surgeons who implant a tube into the groin artery of the stricken Savior and then, without any cutting, into the tissues of His blocked carotid artery. *Reuben's Mandrakes*

fettle: in Metallurgy, loose sand or crushed ore that lines the hearth of a reverberatory furnace before molten metal is poured. *Here Be Dragons*

fireflash: divine illumination. Cf. Luke 17.24: "'like the lightning-flash that lights up the earth from end to end, will the Son of Man be when his day comes.'" *The Atom of the Word*

flavors like a charm: The *charm* quark (a.k.a. "charmed") is but one of six *flavors* or varieties of quarks (hypothetical subatomic particles), the others being down, up, strange, bottom, and top. *Himalayan*

Foliate pebble: In *Mysterium Coniunctionis*, Jung explains that the alchemists connected the "inwards of the head" to "the *terra alba foliata* (foliated [i.e., leafy or layered] white earth), which in this case would be the brain," the so-called "abode of the divine part" (435). Jung adds that the alchemists also connected the "white stone" to Rev. 2.17: "and I will give him a white pebble [. . .] and upon the pebble a new name written, which no one knows except him who receives it" (436n260). In *Thru the Bible with J. Vernon McGee*, vol. 5 (Nashville: Nelson, 1983), McGee weighs an interpretation of the latter passage even more bracing than that of the alchemists: "the people of Asia Minor to whom John was writing had a custom of giving to intimate friends a *tessera*, a cube or rectangular block of stone or ivory, with words or symbols engraved on it. It was a secret, private possession of the one who received it. [Thus,] Christ says that He is going to give to each of His own a stone with a new name engraved upon it. I do not believe that it will be a new name for you and me but that it will be a new name for *Him*. I believe that each name will be different because He means something different to each one of us. It will be His personal and intimate name to each of us" (909). *The Foliate Pebble*

Forever dying: In *Alchemical Studies*, Jung characterizes the *lapis*, the self-realized individual, as "a being that is forever dying yet eternal" (259). *Hieroglyph*

freehold: a life estate; here, the world retained by God for His own use. *Cinderdust*

From all nations chosen: Cf. Matt. 28.19: "'Go forth therefore and make all nations my disciples [. . .].'" *Technical Jesus*

Fruit of the rhizome: a reference to the inverted (metallic) world-tree that unites "the powers of Above and Below," the roots of its ores upraised in the air and its head or summit planted in the earth (Jung, *Alchemical Studies* 233, 311). In Gnostic literature, "the tree symbolizes a living process as well as a process of enlightenment" (313-14). See also Jung's comment on the gist of his own empiric speculations: "The psychology of the unconscious has to reckon with long periods of time [. . .] compared with which the individual is no more than the passing blossom and fruit of the rhizome [the plant stem] under-ground" (90). *Self-Similar*

funnelweb: the filmy network either of the Milky Way Galaxy or of the Funnel-web Mygalomorph, a "dangerously poisonous spider" that catches insects "by entangling them in a sheet of silk. The spider hides in a tube in one corner of the sheet" (Herbert W. Levi and Lorna R. Levi, *A Guide to Spiders and Their Kin* [New York: Golden, 1968] 16, 24). *Heuristic; Planet of the Body*

furrow: In rebirth myths, the *furrow* or cleft in the soil often "stands for a woman" (Jung, *Symbols of Transformation* 340). *Hybrid; Rebis*

Gaea's cauldron keyholed: The expanding big bang cosmos produces (in addition to *soma* [body] and *pneuma* [spirit]) an opening for a key—a vital or essential entity not unlike the soul. Gaea (in Greek mythology, the Goddess of Earth) is seen here as the Supreme Mother of *all* life. See Baring and Cashford, *The Myth of the Goddess* 304. *Cinderdust*

Gaea's helix: DNA, the hereditary molecule, double-stranded and spiral-shaped. *Reuben's Mandrake*

Gaea's sapphirine blossom: the *lapis*, or "sapphirine flower," of alchemy. In *Alchemical Studies*, Jung mentions that "The special virtue of the sapphire is that it endows its wearer with chastity, piety, and constancy." In addition, "It was used as a medicament for comforting the heart" (258-59). See also Jung, *Psychology and Alchemy* 80, including fig. 30: "the 'golden flower of alchemy' [. . .] can sometimes be a blue flower: 'The sapphire blue flower of the hermaphrodite.'" *Dancing in the Dark*

galeated: covered with a helmet. *The Autonomous Android; Holons*

Gamonymous His side and then a cloth: In *Alchemical Studies*, Jung defines the Greek term "gamonymus" as "a kind of chymical wedding, [. . .] an indissoluble, hermaphroditic union [of Sol and Luna]" (136). *Gamonymous*, the adjectival form adopted here, alludes to the marriage not only of Adam and Eve at the Creation, but also of Christ and His bride (the Church as well as Mary) at the foot of the Cross. The *cloth* is the seamless tunic of the crucified Christ, a garment "woven in one piece throughout" (John 19.24) and offered to His followers either as an emblem of perfect wholeness or as a wedding gift to His bride. *Citizen of the Cosmos*

Garment from Edom: the blood-soaked tunic of the prefigured Christian Savior. Cf. Isa. 63.1: "'Who is this coming from Edom, / coming from Bozrah, his garments stained red?'" *Orbifold*

Gemini: here, not only the zodiacal constellation located in the Northern Hemisphere, but also the human counterparts of its two brightest stars, Castor and Pollux. *On the Care and Feeding of Robots*

Gender instantiated, spouses fast: the hermaphrodite as an expression of the unified and coherent wholeness of the individual. In *Mysterium Coniunctionis*, Jung indicates that "Adam must have had two faces, in accordance with [the Rabbinic] interpretation of Psalm 139.5: 'Thou hast beset me behind and before' [. . .]" (408). In *Aion*, Jung adds that "The splitting of the Original Man into husband and wife expresses an act of nascent consciousness; it gives birth to a pair of opposites, thereby making consciousness possible" (204). In other words, "individuation is a 'mysterium coniunctionis,' the self being experienced as a nuptial union of opposite halves [. . .]" (64). *Citizen of the Cosmos*

Ge's hypertext: the secrets of the cosmos compared to links of data that reside within related Web pages. Ge, a variant form of Gaea, is both the Greek Goddess of Earth and the Supreme Mother of *all* life. *Heuristic*

Ge's inner firmament: According to Paracelsus [AD 1493-1541], "The shining body is the [holistic] *corpus astrale*, the 'firmament' or 'star' in man" (Jung, *Alchemical Studies* 152). *Eve's Microchip*

Ge's technical Jesus: a bionic human; a silicon hybrid, with its embedded brain—the prototype of the new, postbiological, genetically enhanced, digitally programmed Christian coheir. (In 2002, James McLean Ledford, a Christian transhumanist, created a Web site whose Internet domain name is *technical-jesus.com*.) *Technical Jesus*

glaived: equipped with a broadsword. The astronaut surfaces here as an heroic coheir of Christ. *Template*

glue: gum arabic, or "blessed" red gum, "the [alchemical] medium between mind and body and the union of both" (Jung, *Psychology and Alchemy* 161, 401). *The Autonomous Android; Mindlinks; Tattoo*

the god through the lap: In *Symbols of Transformation*, Jung, quoting the Christian theologian Clement of Alexandria (c. AD 150-215), observes that "the symbol of the Sabazius mysteries [a variant of the Mithraic mysteries] was 'The god through the lap: and that is a snake which is dragged through the laps of the initiates.'" According to Jung, an Orphic hymn that describes a similar ritual "suggests that the god [Bacchus] entered his devotees as if through the female genitals" (343). *Churning-Stick*

Going nowhere I have nowhere to go: an echo of the heroine's muted yet chilling lament in the 20th-Century Fox film version of *Jane Eyre* (1944): "Going nowhere, I had nowhere to go." The latter statement itself is a paraphrase of the titular character's complaint in Charlotte Bronte's novel: "What was I to do? Where to go? Oh, intolerable questions, when I could do nothing and go nowhere!" ([1848; New York: Bantam, 1981] 308). In John Houseman and Aldous Huxley's revised screenplay (February 2, 1943), the line, interpolated in the film as Jane's despairing voice-over, does not appear. See "SimplyScripts"<simplyscripts.com/genre/drama-scripts.html>. *Hieroglyph*

***Grainy abstract plenum*:** The German philosopher and physicist Gottfried Wilhelm von Leibnitz (AD 1646-1716) believed that space is an infinite unity filled with connected matter. *Grainy Abstract Plenum*

Granum frumenti: the miraculous Bread of Life. See Jung, *Alchemical Studies* 306: "It is not always the fruit of the [sun-and-moon] tree, but of the *granum frumenti*, the grain of wheat, from which the food of immortality is prepared [. . .]." *Cadmus and the Sown Men of Thebes*

***haptic*:** tactile; hence, in Robotics, pertaining to any of several tools or devices that interface the user through the sense of touch. *Hieroglyph; Leprous; Mindlinks; Self-Assembled; Technical Jesus*

***har*:** the Hebrew word for hill or mountain. *The Platonic Man*

***Harranite bleacher*:** a worker from Harran—an ancient city of trade in SE Turkey—who whitens cloth or wool. *Dancing in the Dark*

***Harvests the peacock*:** The dexterous android either reaps or extracts from the alchemical retort "the exquisite display of colours in the peacock's fan," a phenomenon that heralds, symbolically, not only "the imminent synthesis of all qualities and elements" (Jung, *Mysterium Coniunctionis* 290), but also the attainment of psychological wholeness. *The Robot Not Yet Human*

Having waxed with Luna into the sun: Both in its ascent to Heaven and in its subsequent descent to Earth, the soul experiences its philosophical transformation—from body into spirit, and then from spirit into body again—by "waxing in Luna into the nature of the sun" (Jung, *Mysterium Coniunctionis* 220n546). *Self-Assembled*

***He actuates his eyes till muscles spread*:** The rotary actuators—the motors that animate the humanoid robot—function like *muscles* and joints, while a separate optical device—an image chip—integrates the pixels of his gaze. *The Atom of the Word*

heart of flesh: Cf. Ezek. 36.26: "I will give you a new heart and put a new spirit within you; I will take the heart of stone from your body and give you a heart of flesh." *Heart of Flesh*

***heated discus thrown*:** Warmed by the sun, the planet Earth spins in space like a flat, circular plate. *Arecibo's Dish*

***Heaven's swain*:** the Spirit of Christ, suitor as well as shepherd of His believer-priests. *Silverfoot*

***Heaven the third*:** the Holy Ghost, the *third* Person in the Trinity. *The Atom of the Word*

***Hebrew seamster*:** a maker of the "appointments of the Tabernacle [of the Tokens]" (Exod. 38.21) and of "the sacred vestments for Aaron the priest" and for his sons when "they minister as priests" (Exod. 39.41). *Dancing in the Dark*

***Hecate's precincts*:** In Greek mythology, Hecate, a "spook goddess of night and phantoms," guards the gate of Hades (Jung, *Symbols of Transformation* 369). *The Atom of the Word*

He climbs the heights with captives in his train: Cf. Eph. 4.7-8: "each of us has been given his gift, his due portion of Christ's bounty. Therefore Scripture says: 'He ascended into the heights / with captives in his train; / he gave gifts to men.'" *Silverfoot*

he [. . .] / Creates the taste by which he is enjoyed: Cf. Ralph Waldo Emerson, "Spiritual Laws," in *Emerson's Essays*, introd. Irwin Edman (1926; New York: Apollo-Crowell, 1961) 100-01: "Each man has his own vocation. [. . .] He creates the taste by which he is enjoyed. He provokes the wants to which he can minister. By doing his own work he unfolds himself." *Spiritual Laws*

***He is the door*:** Cf. John 10.9: "'I am the door; anyone who comes into the fold through me shall be safe.'" *Orbifold*

***He networks the cosmos*:** With cables, bridges, routers, and switches, the "Sown man" wires the world in order to share as well as to access information. *Himalayan*

***Hephaestus*:** in ancient Greek literature, both the lame god of fire, metals and metallurgy and the husband of Aphrodite. *The Autonomous Android; Here Be Dragons; Mindlinks; Orphan; Quintessence; Self-Similar; Spiritual Laws*

***He pours from His fire like molten metal*:** Cf. Jung's description of the Son of Man in Rev. 1.15: "the feet stand in the fire and glow like molten metal" (*Mysterium Coniunctionis* 441). *Here Be Dragons*

***Heracles' arrows pierce us*:** an allusion not only to Chiron and Pholus, centaurs accidentally wounded by Heracles' (or Hercules') poisoned arrow shafts, but also to the iconic unicorn—here, a substitute for Jesus—lanced in the lap of the Virgin Mary. (See Jung, *Psychology and Alchemy*, figs. 241 and 242.) Jung shapes a different interpretation of the same emblem in *Symbols of Transformation*: "The deadly arrows do not strike the hero from without; it is [he] himself who hunts, fights, and tortures himself." Hence, "the meaning of this 'piercing' is clear: it is the act of union with oneself, a sort of self-fertilization, and also a self-violation, a self-murder [...]" (291-92). *Churning-Stick*

Her crescent foetus: Gaea's waxing moonchild. *Arecibo's Dish*

Here Be Dragons: the translation of a Latin phrase—*hic sunt dracones*—used by sixteenth-century European mapmakers to signify unknown or perilous terrain. *Here Be Dragons*

Hermes: the Greek god who served as messenger, scribe, and herald for the other gods. *Hieroglyph; Himalayan; Hybrid; Leprous; Technical Jesus*

Hermes' syzygy: In medieval alchemy, Hermes (or Mercurius), in his role as hermaphroditic *rebis*, combines—i.e., *integrates*—paired opposites. Thus, in *The Archetypes and the Collective Unconscious*, trans. R. F. C. Hull (1959; Princeton: Princeton UP, 1990), C. G. Jung suggests that, although "the original hermaphrodite type [...] seems to go far back into prehistory" (69n27), in modern psychological parlance, "The hermaphrodite means nothing less than a union of the strongest and most striking opposites. [. . .] As civilization develops, the bisexual primordial being turns into a symbol of the unity of personality, a symbol of the self, where the war of opposites finds peace. In this way the primordial being becomes the distant goal of man's self-development, having been from the very beginning a projection of his unconscious wholeness" (173-75). (For a startling illustration of the alchemical hermaphrodite, see Jung, *Psychology and Alchemy* 244, fig. 125.) *Hieroglyph*

He sits in the moon and goes round with it: Jung notes that "in Plutarch [c. AD 46-120] Hermes [god of revelation and guide of souls] sits in the moon and goes round with it (just as Heracles does in the sun)." In effect, the *moon* is the white "receptacle of souls" (*Mysterium Coniunctionis* 140). *Eve's Microchip*

He sits like a shade, a man in his booth: Cf. Søren Kierkegaard, *The Sickness unto Death*, trans. Alastair Hannay (1849; Penguin, 1989) 157: "The man sitting in a glass case is not so constrained as is each human being in his transparency before God." *The Cheshire of Sense*

He swallows his body into his head: Ouroboros, "the dragon [that] devours himself from the tail upwards until his whole body has been swallowed into his head" (Jung, *Mysterium Coniunctionis* 117). For the alchemists, the mercurial dragon symbolizes the "circulatory process" that leads to life, self-fertilization, and rebirth (365). *Here Be Dragons*

Heuristic: in Computer Science, using step-by-step, rule-of-thumb techniques in order to find solutions to problems. *Heuristic*

He vitrifies my helmet: Christ solidifies the transparency of the astronaut's (plastic) bubble helmet. The reference to vitrification—the conversion into glass—is Hermetic. Thus, in *Alchemical Studies*, Jung explains that "For Zosimos [3rd cent. AD] and the later alchemists the head had the meaning of the 'omega element' or 'round element' [. . .], a synonym for the arcane or transformative substance" (72). See also Jung's description of the Philosopher's stone as "the Chemical King," as "the king descending from Heaven," and as "a tall and helmeted man (homo galeatus et altus)," in *Mysterium Coniunctionis* 263n21. *Cinderdust*

Hidden Sagittarius, hindsight's ace: a constellation located in the direction of our Galaxy's center and covered with clusters of stars and clouds. In the night sky, *Sagittarius*, the Archer, aims his bow at the heart of another constellation, Scorpius, or the Scorpion. However, here, *Sagittarius* is dubbed *hindsight's ace* (belated wisdom's expert) because, in Greek mythology, he is sometimes identified with Chiron, the immortal centaur who, having been accidentally wounded by Hercules, conquers the scorpion by *choosing* to die. According to the ancient symbolists, the latter beast of prey embodies both an ideogram of evil and a "reservoir and instrument of death" (Charbonneau-Lassay, *The Bestiary of Christ* 342). *Planet of the Body*

Hieroglyph or number: a reference both to the self-born, ring-shaped dragon Ouroboros, "the hieroglyph of Eternity" (Jung, *Alchemical Studies* 259), and to the binary digit 0 itself, still another numinous symbol of wholeness. *Transconscious*

Himalayan: supracelestial. Cf. Jung, *Alchemical Studies* 312: "Krishna says in the Bhagavadgita (ch. 15): 'I am the Himalaya among mountains and the *ashvattha* [the seat of the gods] among trees.'" *Himalayan*

His brazen serpent: the bronze *serpent* that Moses erected at Yahweh's command as a prefiguration of the salvific Christ. See Num. 21.4-9. *Here Be Dragons*

His Father's "branch of Mine": Cf. John 15.1-4: "'I am the real vine, and my Father is the gardener. Every barren branch of mine he cuts away; and every fruiting branch he cleans, to make it more fruitful still. [. . .] No branch can bear fruit by itself, but only if it remains united with the vine; no more can you bear fruit, unless you remain united with me.'" *Orbifold*

His fingers flexed, articulated, fed: While celebrating Mass, the dexterous humanoid robot has received, and eaten, the Bread of Heaven. *The Atom of the Word*

His headpiece like Carmel: Robonaut's saffron acrylic helmet compared to the Shulamite's "lustrous" ribboned tresses in The Song of Songs 7.5: "You carry your head like Carmel." In the Old Testament, *Carmel* is a region rich with arable lands and blossoming vineyards, like the Garden of Eden. *Himalayan*

His herald's scepter: the instrumented holding rod that the telemanipulated android has learned to grip with a gloved hand and to insert into a socket. Here, Robonaut is likened to Hermes, the Greek precursor and messenger of the gods. See the photographs of NASA's robotic astronaut in "Robonaut Activity Report," *Robonaut*, May 2003, NASA, 4 August 2007 <http://robonaut.jsc.nasa.gov/status/May_Robonaut_

Status_03.htm>. *Leprous*

His model but a centaur: i.e., Chiron, in Greek and Roman mythology, the wisest *centaur* (half-man, half-horse]—the benevolent teacher of Asclepius, Heracles (Hercules), and Achilles. *Silverfoot*

his nodding head: After he reads the Communion verse, the autonomous android reverently lowers and then raises his *head*. Cf. Peter James and Nick Thorpe, *Ancient Inventions* (New York: Ballantine, 1994) 136: The Egyptians had arranged "'marvels' in their temples such as statues with nodding heads and concealed speaking tubes that gave the illusion of talking gods." *The Atom of the Word*

His shining body: According to the alchemists, "in man there is a shining body, the radical moisture, which comes from the sphere of the heavenly waters [. . .] and is the 'firmament' or 'star' in man" (Jung, *Alchemical Studies* 151-52). *Robonaut*

His spread: not only the spatiotemporal body and blood of Christ—the Incarnate Word—upraised and glorified on the Cross (John 17.1-26), but also the Mystical Body and Blood of Christ elevated and consecrated in the Holy Sacrifice of the Mass. *Citizen of the Cosmos*

His unit haptic: the MMU (Manned Maneuvering Unit)—the backpack propulsion system that the untethered shuttle astronaut operates during satellite repair and recovery (Herrod, *Space Walks* 46-49). The astronaut uses his fingertips to manipulate the system's right and left hand controllers. Deemed risky, the MMU has not been piloted since the Challenger disaster in 1986. *Leprous*

holon: a whole embedded in larger wholes; hence, an entity—whether an atom or a universe—that is both a whole and a part. Arthur Koestler coined the term in *The Ghost in the Machine* (1967; New York: Arkana-Penguin, 1990) 48. *Cadmus and the Sown Men of Thebes; Canonical; Heart of Flesh; Hieroglyph; Himalayan; Holons; On the Care and Feeding of Robots; Pulse of Glory; Quintessence; Rebis; Screen; Seminal; A Single Day*

Horn of End-time: in Rev. 11.15, the trumpet of the unidentified seventh angel who announces Judgment Day. *Heuristic*

Hosea's yeast: a two-sided symbol of the *yeast* of iniquity and the leaven of redemption that evokes the divine marriage of the Old Testament prophet Hosea to "wanton" Gomer (and, by extension, of Yahweh to sinful Israel) and of the Risen Lamb to His sealed Church. See Hos. 1.2-3 and 7.4. *Window*

Hubbles spy: after Edwin Hubble (AD 1889-1953), an American astronomer who discovered, along with other astronomers, that the universe is expanding; hence, spacecraft telescopes that observe—and transmit optical images of—the Milky Way Galaxy. *Self-Similar*

Human beings, with God born into them: Cf. Ron Kangas, "The Serpent and the

Bride: The Recovery of the Highest Gospel," *Affirmation & Critique* 5.1 (2000): 25: "It is surely the greatest wonder in the universe that human beings—fallen, sinful, satanified human beings—can be born of God to become children of God. Today many are seeking signs, wonders, and miracles, but they do not realize that there is no greater miracle than regeneration. What miracle could be greater than the divine birth, the birth of human beings through regeneration to become God-men, human beings with God born into them?" *Self-Similar*

hyacinthine master: a reference to the sapphire blue flower of alchemy as birthplace of the *filius philosophorum* and to the speaker as heavenly adept. See Jung, *Psychology and Alchemy* 80, including fig. 30. *The Foliate Pebble*

hyacinthine matrix: not only the sapphire-blue sky, "the vessel of divine germination" (Jung, *Psychology and Alchemy* 237n16), but also "the indeterminable divine nature [. . .] of the self" (19). *Arecibo's Dish*

Hyaline: clear; transparent; glassy. *The Platonic Man*

hybrid of the dew: the first Adam, the "true" hermaphroditic microcosm, "who bore his invisible Eve hidden in his body" (Jung, *Psychology and Alchemy* 319n2). In alchemy, the *dew* is but one of innumerable names for the "unknown substance," the *prima materia* (317, 320). *Tattoo*

hypercube: a cube in four dimensions; unraveled, it becomes a three-dimensional, "crosslike tesseract" (Michio Kaku, *Hyperspace* [New York: Oxford UP, 1994] 70-71). *Cadmus and the Sown Men of Thebes; Orbifold; Seminal*

hyperspace: "higher-dimensional space"—according to superstring theory, "the three dimensions of space (length, width, and breadth) and one of time [. . .] extended by six more spatial dimensions" (Kaku, *Hyperspace* vii-viii). *Cadmus and the Sown Men of Thebes; The Novenary Foetus; Orbifold; Tattoo*

hyphenate: a person, place, or thing of mixed origin or identity. *Arecibo's Dish; The Autonomous Android; Canonical; Citizen of the Cosmos; Dancing in the Dark; Grainy Abstract Plenum; Quintessence; Reuben's Mandrakes; Seminal*

Hyphenate indwelt: The speaker, being Spirit-filled, belongs to both Heaven and Earth. *Grainy Abstract Plenum*

Hypostatized, we meditate the scheme: an allusion to the "baptism of power" that Andrew Murray explores in *The Spirit of Christ*. The inner light of the body having been reified by the Spirit of the glorified Jesus "poured out at Pentecost," we may now reflect upon "what previously had no existence—a life at once human and divine" (82-83). *Arecibo's Dish*

ichor: in Greek mythology, the ethereal fluid of the gods; here, the transubstantiated Eucharistic wine, a metonym for Christ. *The Atom of the Word; Mindlinks*

I have heard His voice and have seen His shape: Cf. John 5.37 (AV) in Jung, *Mysterium Coniunctionis* 437: "'We have heard his voice, but we have not seen his shape.'" *Orphan*

Illustrates* (il-LUS-trates) *his secret, suffused with snow: With the archetypal symbol of the snow-flecked crow, the Christian coheir momentarily illuminates one of those inexplicable "creative processes that can be truly grasped only by experience, though intellect may give them a name." See Jung, *Psychology and Alchemy* 482, especially fig. 269: "The artifex and his *soror mystica* making the gesture of the secret at the end of the [alchemical] work." *Mindlinks*

Imprint of the Spirit, heart's pilaster: the supportive Holy *Spirit* that indwells the heart of each coheir of the Kingdom and that the speaker likens to a reinforced column that projects from a wall. Cf. the idea found in Michael Maier, *De circulo physico quadrato* (Oppenheim, 1616) and paraphrased in Jung, *Psychology and Alchemy* 343: "Little by little the sun has imprinted its image on the earth, and that image is the gold. The sun is the image of God, the heart [as seat of the soul] is the sun's image in man, just as gold is the sun's image in the earth (also called *Deus terrenus*), and God is known in the gold." *The Foliate Pebble*

in bucket or bin: In order to retrieve a rogue communications satellite, the astronaut stands with his feet strapped to a manipulator foot restraint (a "cherry picker") that juts out from the shuttle orbiter's crane arm and that looks not unlike the hydraulic-lift platform attached to a telephone lineman's bucket truck. See Kerrod, *Space Walks* 49-50. *Leprous*

Infrared transceivers: in the distributed sensor network of a mobile robot, a device that combines transmitting and receiving functions via infrared technology. *Earthshine*

In himself is his might: Cf. Emerson, "Spiritual Laws," in *Emerson's Essays* 102: "What a man does, that he has. [...] In himself is his might." *Spiritual Laws*

In its egg the sunpoint: in the guise of light or fire, the Godhead represented by the alchemists as "the world's centre" (Jung, *Mysterium Coniunctionis* 45-47). *Self-Similar*

in quicksilver gird: The astronaut clothes himself in a suit of liquid metal, "the wonderful substance [...] which glistens and animates within" (Jung, *Psychology and Alchemy* 292). *The Atom of the Word*

The instrumented staff with which I knock: the metal rod sensed by the gloved fingertip load cells of NASA's dexterous Robonaut. *Hieroglyph*

interface: in Computer Science, the point of interaction between adjacent entities, including a software program, a hardwire device, and a human operator. *Mindlinks; Seminal; Technical Jesus*

***interface, then plumb, / Transmit the Spirit*:** The robot almost human seeks not only to integrate both his body and his soul with the indwelling *Spirit* of Christ, but also to access, measure, and then impart the power of the "Holiest of All," the coded witness in the user interface. See Murray, *The Spirit of Christ* 208-10. *Seminal*

Intermezzi: brief psychic episodes construed as transmundane cerebral insertions. In the work of medieval alchemists, "dreams and dream visions are often mentioned as important intermezzi or as sources of revelation" (Jung, *Psychology and Alchemy* 252). *Arecibo's Dish*

***In the air rooted, summits in the lea / Torn out of the earth*:** in Hermetic philosophy, the inverted Tree of the Metals regarded as a symbol of the self. Cf. Jung, *Alchemical Studies* 311, where Laurentius Ventura, the sixteenth-century alchemist, notes not only that "'The roots of its ores are in the air and the summits in the earth,'" but also that, like the mythical mandrake, it "shrieks when it is torn out of the earth." *Himalayan*

***in the fissure vaster*:** In *Alchemical Studies,* Jung observes that, according to Paracelsus, in the human skull, "there is an 'aquastric fissure,' in men on the forehead, in women at the back of the head," and that, of all the Paracelsan ideas," the [celestial] Aquaster [i.e., the quasi-material 'water star'] comes closest to the modern concept of the unconscious" (139-40). The speaker is *in the fissure vaster* because the latter groove relates him telepathically to the spiritual world—even "to phenomena or events indicative of the future" (139n34). *The Foliate Pebble*

Intuits the space: Instinctively, the telepresent *human* operator apprehends, even as he controls, the actions of his robotic partner. Hans Moravec describes the experience in *Robot: Mere Machine to Transcendent Mind* (New York: Oxford UP, 1999): "Images from the robot's two camera eyes appear on your eyeglass viewscreens [. . .]. Your movements [animate] the robot in exact synchrony." With contacts on your skin, "When you reach for something in the viewscreens, the robot grasps it and [through its instrumented surface and chemical sensors] relays to your muscles and skin the resulting weight, shape, texture, and temperature, creating the perfect illusion that you inhabit the robot's body" (168-69). *The Atom of the Word*

***Invests my astronaut*:** [Christ] clothes or arrays His new disciple in the symbols of earthly power and heavenly authority. *Cinderdust*

***iris of consciousness*:** the membrane of the eye through whose dilated pupil light passes—here, as the messenger of God. *Pulse of Glory*

***I stood on the chaos*:** the self-transforming speaker as Anthropos, *rebis,* Mercurius, and/or Christ, standing on the globe, i.e., the round *chaos.* See Jung, *Psychology and Alchemy,* figs. 64, 125, 164, and 199. *The Foliate Pebble*

***its iridescent case*:** a truncated alchemical conceit. The white brain-pan that encloses the consciousness of each subject (Gaea, the personified Earth, as well as the human speaker) contains the many colors or "secrets" of the rainbow. Thus, for the medieval alchemist, when molecular separation and, symbolically, psychic disunity are overcome, "all of the colours of the world will appear," a sublime neural activity of the brain that "points, as it were, to a coming of God, or even to his presence" (Jung, *Mysterium Coniunctionis* 288). *Arecibo's Dish*

Its skein but a screen: the speaker's take on concepts developed by Gilles Deleuze in *The Fold: Leibniz and the Baroque*, trans. Tom Conley (1988; Minneapolis: U of Minnesota P, 1993) and, with Felix Guattari, in *A Thousand Plateaus: Capitalism and Schizophrenia*, trans. Brian Massumi (Minneapolis: U of Minnesota P, 1987)—in effect, not only the "striated" net of "rhizomatic" space, but also the pleated membrane of the human cerebrum, through or on which events (qualities, figures, things) issue from chaos. In *A Thousand Plateaus*, Deleuze imagines that, in smooth, "nomadic" space, the perceiver deterritorializes the enclosed, "sedentary" grid of the world in order to redistribute it into an infinite succession of "haptic" topologies and "local absolutes" (380-82). *Screen*

jade in the burse: the Communion wafer carried in the pyx, the latter vessel itself contained in a leather purse. In this stanza, both transubstantiated Host and reified sun-moon child are likened to *jade*, the androgynous royal gem of China symbolic of wisdom, courage, compassion, and beauty. *Pulse of Glory*

jasper: a gemstone, light-green or yellow. Cf. John's description of "the holy city of Jerusalem" in Rev. 21.11: "it had the radiance of some priceless jewel, like a jasper, clear as crystal." In fact, "The wall was built of jasper, while the city itself was of pure gold [...]" (Rev. 21.18). *Window*

Jesus' foal: the donkey foal on which Jesus made His triumphant entrance into Jerusalem. See Matt. 21.1-5 and also Zech. 9.9. *Canonical*

jew's-harp: a musical instrument composed of a small metal frame held between the teeth and a flexible metal frame plucked with the fingers. Musical effects can be enhanced by the use of additional tongues. Cf. "Spiritual Laws," in *Emerson's Essays* 102: Praising various nineteenth-century virtuosi, Emerson remarks that "[Niccolo] Paganini can extract rapture from a catgut, and [Karl] Eulenstein from a jew's-harp [...]." *Spiritual Laws*

jinn: in popular usage, a single supernatural being that can assume either human or animal form. *Himalayan; Robonaut*

Kevlar: a brand name for a heat-resistant, synthetic fiber used in making the padded body of Robonaut, NASA's humanoid astronaut. *Cadmus and the Sown Men of Thebes; Himalayan*

knights of faith: NASA's shuttle astronauts imaged as Christ's coheirs, a retake on Kierkegaard's balletic *knights of faith* (and hence of infinite resignation) in *Fear and Trembling*: "One does not need to see them in the air; one needs only to see them the instant [that] they touch and have touched the earth—and then one recognizes them. But to be able to come down in such a way that instantaneously one seems to stand and to walk, to change the leap into life into walking, absolutely to express the sublime in the pedestrian—[. . .] this is the one and only marvel" (*Fear and Trembling/Repetition* 41). *Eve's Microchip*

A lace and then a face: Christ's imprint on Veronica's sudary. *Citizen of the Cosmos*

Lace like a lattice: the fabric of Spacetime likened to the sticky weave of spider silk. *Orbifold*

lammergeier's wight: the lamblike Christ—a *wight* or living being—pictured as the prey of the satanic lammergeier, the sheep vulture. *The Cheshire of Sense*

the land of Nod: After he had killed his brother Abel and become "a vagrant and a wanderer on earth, [. . .] Cain went out from the Lord's presence and settled in the land of Nod to the east of Eden" (Gen. 4.14-16). *Transconscious*

The Lantern with Two Lights: the transfigured self described by the alchemists as the "light of sun *and* moon"—i.e., the sun-moon child (Jung, *Mysterium Coniunctionis* 220n547). *The Lantern with Two Lights*

Leibnitz' monads: For the German philosopher and mathematician Gottfried Wilhelm von Leibnitz (AD 1646-1716), the monad was the basic unit of matter—in Jungian terms, the symbol of an "interior microcosm," the collective unconscious, that is "identical in all individuals and is therefore *one*" and whole (Jung, *Aion* 164). *Canonical*

leprous: an alchemical epithet—either impure, unclean, contaminated, or corrupt, like "metals, oxides, and salts" (Jung, *Alchemical Studies* 290n6). *The Autonomous Android; Cinderdust; Heuristic; Hieroglyph; Leprous; Self-Assembled; Self-Similar; A Single Day*

Leprous as Hephaestus: Because of his physical defects—rust and verdigris, the symptoms of his metal's sickness—the autonomous android, like the lame god of metallurgy, may not attain the spiritual unity that he seeks. *The Autonomous Android*

Leviathan baited: the evil "monster of the deep"—either whale, crocodile, or dragon—described in Isa. 27.1. In *Alchemical Studies*, Jung remarks that "in medieval allegory the hook with which God the Father catches the Leviathan is the crucifix." In effect, God uses the second Adam as "bait for catching the powers of darkness" (334). See also *Psychology and Alchemy*, fig. 28. *Window*

lexies: in modern semiotics, sections of arbitrarily coded verbal signs that manifest the *langue* (the underlying linguistic system) that permeates a literary text. *Heuristic*

Life above life, in infinite degrees: With these words from "Experience," Emerson weighs the divine tendencies of the individual. See *Emerson's Essays* 313: "The consciousness in each man is a sliding scale, which identifies him now with the First Cause, and now with the flesh of his body; life above life, in infinite degrees." *Holons*

Light's metabolized screeds: The spiritually indwelt Christian absorbs like material food both the Eucharistic Host and testamentary revelation. Cf. Gal. 2.20: "I have been crucified with Christ: the life I now live is not my life, but the life which Christ lives in me [...]." *Here Be Dragons*

Like Mars and Venus, concrete as a thumb: a nod not only to the archetypal pair of opposites—male and female—entwined in the net of Vulcan, but also to the psychological wholeness generated by their union. Here, the phallic *thumb* "represents the libido, or psychic energy in its creative aspect" (Jung, *Symbols of Transformation* 124). *The Foliate Pebble*

***lisible*:** The speaker perceives the world as a readerly (or readable) text, one that is open-ended, playful, and joyful. See Roland Barthes' use of the term in *S/Z*, trans. Richard Miller (1970; New York: Hill-Farrar, 1974) 4-6: In a "readerly," i.e., an "absolutely plural," text, "the networks are many and interact without any of them being able to surpass the rest; this text is a galaxy of signifiers, not a structure of signifieds; [...] the codes [that] it mobilizes extend as far as the eye can reach [...]." *Pulse of Glory*

***a lizard in the flame*:** in Hermetic texts, a symbol of heavenly transformation—"The Mercurial spirit of the *prima materia*, in the shape of a salamander, frolicking in the fire" (Jung, *Psychology and Alchemy* 276, fig. 138). *Robonaut*

***lodestar*:** a guide star—an alternating fixed point in the sky, like Polaris, Thuban, and Vega—used to chart or navigate one's way. *Grainy Abstract Plenum*

***mandrake*:** the root of the mandragora, a medicinal plant, formerly thought to possess occult powers because of its seeming resemblance to the human body—specifically, to a man standing upside down. *Heuristic; Reuben's Mandrakes; The Robot Not Yet Human; Self-Similar*

Manikin: here, either an homunculus, the preformed human supposedly present in the sperm cell; or a creative dwarf—like the dactyl and the thumbling, an infantile chthonic god; or, simply enough, a life-size model of the human body (Jung, *Symbols of Transformation* 127). *Leprous; The Platonic Man*

***manikin's case*:** the outer torso shell—with both "a custom-fitted fabric skin" and "a subcutaneous layer of foam padding"—that covers Robonaut's aluminum endoskeleton. See "Robonaut – Body," *Robonaut*, NASA, 19 July 2007 <http.://robonaut.jsc.nasa.gov/body.htm>. *Leprous*

A man is a method: Emerson's testament to the primacy of the totalistic self and one of the unifying themes in this book. See "Spiritual Laws," in *Emerson's Essays* 103: "A man is a method, a progressive arrangement; a selecting principle, gathering his like to him wherever he goes." *Window*

manna that we swish / Spirit-generated: the miraculous food of the Eucharist, the Host mixed with wine that Christian communicants *swish* or move in the mouth with a gurgling sound. *Arecibo's Dish*

mare: a dark plain on the Earth's moon. The word is pronounced MAH-ray. *Here Be Dragons; Holons: Quintessence; Rebis*

Maria's blossom: in the alchemical retort, the fruit-laden flower of the myrtle, one of several names for the philosophical tree. Maria Prophetissa, perhaps *the* archetypal Hermetic sage, called the branches of the myrtle "the golden rungs" (286). *Reuben's Mandrakes*

Maria's vase: For Maria Prophetissa, the reputed sister of Moses, "the whole secret of the [alchemist's] art lay in knowledge of the Hermetic vessel," which was both round and divine "and had been hidden from man by the wisdom of the Lord" (Jung, *Alchemical Studies* 85). *Leprous*

Maya: in Hinduism, the illusory world of matter personified as a woman. *The Foliate Pebble*

maydew: according to the Swiss physician and alchemist Paracelsus, "a heavenly food [that] assists sublimation" (Jung, *Alchemical Studies* 153n93). *Arecibo's Dish*

Meal at Emmaus: At "a village called Emmaus," after His death and resurrection, Jesus broke bread with two of His apostles (Luke 24.28-30). *Arecibo's Dish*

mechatronic: pertaining to a fusion of various technologies—especially mechanical, electronic, and computer engineering—that aim to develop as well as to control intelligent machines. *Himalayan; Self-Assembled; Seminal*

Memory's alloy: Shape Memory Alloy, a smart metal—commonly, a mixture of nickel, titanium, and copper—that can actuate a robotic hand. In effect, the metal, "heated and cooled repeatedly" to obtain its force, "remembers" its predetermined shape after being bent. See Kathryn J. DeLaurentis and Constantinos Mavroidis, "Mechanical design of a shape memory alloy actuated prosthetic hand," *Technology and Health Care* 10.2 (2002): 92, IOS Press, 16 July 2007 <http://www.edu.neu.edu/Research/robots/papers/THC.pdf>. *Heuristic*

Metallic coheir: the new scion of the Kingdom of Heaven, a bionic human enhanced with electromechanical body parts. *The Atom of the Word*

Metal on metal, at Advent we wreathe: During *Advent*, a pre-Christmas liturgical season that anticipates even as it celebrates the Coming of the Lord, many Christians fashion *metal* wreaths whose circular shapes symbolize eternal life. *A Single Day*

metal supreme: an elliptical nominative absolute—*metal* [being] *supreme* or ultimate. *The Autonomous Android*

Migrant yet hyphenated: the astronaut construed as a wanderer belonging to both Heaven and Earth. *Citizen of the Cosmos*

millipedes: crawling arthropods with multiple body segments and pairs of legs, often found under rocks or logs or in forest litter. *The Cheshire of Sense*

mindlinks: recurrent, associative neural networks designed in the embodied robot as levels, or layers, of abstraction—e.g., hardware, firmware, assembly forces, multitasking operating systems, and robust, human-specified control processes. *Mindlinks; Robonaut; Technical Jesus*

Mirror starstuff: According to an ancient Greek schema that appealed to sixteenth-century alchemists, the individual (the little world or microcosm) reflects the universe (the macrocosm). Cf. Sagan, *The Cosmic Connection* 255: "He was the matter of the cosmos, contemplating itself. [. . .] He called himself Man. He was one of the starfolk. And he longed to return to the stars." *Arecibo's Dish*

Mithras in the treetop: an allusion to the tree-birth of an ancient Persian sun-god. See plate XL in Jung, *Symbols of Transformation*, where *Mithras* "is shown with half his body rising from the top of a [natal] tree" (247). *Churning-Stick*

Mixed with the lion, Babylon forsworn: "Since the dawn of the [Christian] Church," the ambivalent *lion* has been both a symbol of Christ and an emblem of the devil (Charbonneau-Lassay, *The Bestiary of Christ* 13). Here, the speaker renounces the infernal nature of the *lion*, along with the depraved condition of *Babylon*. *Seminal*

Möbius' (MER-be-us) strand: a continuous, one-sided geometric surface—a space warp "created by twisting a strip of paper 180 degrees and then gluing the ends together." In effect, "outside and inside are identical" (Kaku, *Hyperspace* 60-61). The "Möbius strip" is named after its deviser, the nineteenth-century German mathematician A. F. Möbius. *Himalayan*

Moist albedo: in alchemy, a symbol of spiritual renewal, "the white state of innocence, which like the moon and a bride awaits the bridegroom" (Jung, *Mysterium Coniunctionis* 132). The medieval alchemists held that the moon "secretes the dew or sap of life" (131). *Here Be Dragons*

Monad: not only the indivisible point—"the jot of the iota"—viewed as a Gnostic emblem of the totalistic man or woman (Jung, *Aion* 218), but also a microcosm that, according to Leibnitz, mirrors the universe. *Canonical; Heart of Flesh; Hieroglyph; Holons; The Platonic Man; Rebis; Self-Similar; Son of One Day*

moonchild: a variant of the new, technical Jesus—here, the spiritual android as a precursor of the mythological higher self "conceived by the sun" in the belly of the moon (Jung, *Mysterium Coniunctionis* 175-76) and married to Christ. *The Atom of the Word; Churning-Stick; Himalayan; Hybrid; The Novenary Foetus*

moonplants: immortal sun-and-moon trees that represent unity and bring salvation. See Jung, *Psychology and Alchemy* 351-52 and also figs. 116 and 188. *The Autonomous Android; Hieroglyph; Quintessence*

Moriah's terrain: in Gen. 22.1-12, the land of Mount Moriah, where Abraham prepared to sacrifice his son Isaac. *Here Be Dragons*

multithreading: in Computer Technology, executing different portions, or threads, of a program concurrently. *Mindlinks*

multiverse: a cosmological concept advanced in 1957 by Hugh Everett, and later by Bryce DeWitt, both of whom argue that "an infinite number of possible universes" (including "myriads of copies" of our local world) comprises but one part of physical reality (Kaku, *Hyperspace* 262-64). *Grainy Abstract Plenum; Self-Similar*

mystagogues: interpreters of religious mysteries. *The Atom of the Word; Churning-Stick*

Nearer to the "I" than even the "I": Cf. the experience of "absolute faith" that Paul Tillich advances in *The Courage to Be* (New Haven: Yale UP, 1952) 185, 187: "The God above the God of theism is present, although hidden, in every divine-human encounter. [Biblical religion and Protestant theology] are aware of the paradoxical character of this encounter. [...] They are aware of speaking to somebody to whom you cannot speak because he is not 'somebody,' of asking somebody of whom you cannot ask anything because he gives or gives not before you ask, of saying 'thou' to somebody who is nearer to the I than the I is to itself. Each of these paradoxes drives the religious consciousness toward a God above the God of theism." *Template*

Nebo's chthonic essence: the God that spoke to Moses "face to face" on Mount Nebo (Deut. 34.10), here projected as a mystical being Who combines "the chthonic [or earthy] principle of the serpent and the aerial principle of the bird" (Jung, *Psychology and Alchemy* 292-93). *Sunship*

nematodes that cling: eelworms attached to stones flung from damp soil. *Reuben's Mandrakes*

nematode trussed: an eelworm, its elongated body either curved, or coiled, or tied. *The Foliate Pebble*

Noah's dove: in Gen. 8.11, the bird that signaled God's reconciliation with Noah's descendants, after the flood, "with a newly plucked olive leaf in her beak." Here, the uniped robot, like the *dove*, becomes an emblematic herald of peace. *Silverfoot*

Noctuid moths: night-flying *moths* with cryptic coloration that matches their habitat and that enables them to elude detection. *The Cheshire of Sense*

nodes in the shin: connection points in a distributed sensor network, an array of incoming data managed in the front part of the humanoid robot's leg. *Earthshine*

Nomads in the mare: wanderers on the surface of a lunar plain. *Here Be Dragons*

noumenon: the essence of an object; in Kantian terms, "the thing in itself" independent of the mind, yet postulated by it. *Robonaut*

novenary foetus: In alchemy, the number nine is a symbol of both the transformation process and the eternal One. See Jung, *Alchemical Studies* 151: "The One is the midpoint of the circle, the centre of the triad, and [. . .] the 'novenary foetus' [. . .]." *The Novenary Foetus*

Obelisk: a shaft of stone—a four-sided pillar—with a tapering pyramidal top; hence, here, both a monolith and a symbol of the human frame. *Sunship*

Olympus Mons on Mars, calderas pursed, / Along the ridge of Tharsis: See Patrick Moore, *Travellers in Space and Time* (New York: Doubleday, 1984) 45: "During the descent to Mars, [. . .] our main attention is focused upon a string of huge shield volcanoes spread out along the ridge, [a chain of mountains] which has been named Tharsis. The loftiest [volcano] of them all is aptly called Olympus Mons or Mount Olympus; it towers to fifteen miles above the ground below, and at its summit there is a 40-mile volcanic crater of the type known as a caldera. Other volcanoes in the Tharsis area are hardly inferior [. . .]," their *calderas* shaped—as in "Grainy Abstract Plenum"—either like a woman's open pouch or like lips *pursed* or puckered into an emphatic "O." *Grainy Abstract Plenum*

omniverse: in current physical cosmology, an infinity of universes—the conglomeration of all possible worlds. *Heuristic; Rebis; Screen; Template*

omphalos: the mid-point or navel of the earth—Golgotha; according to an ancient Christian tradition, both the hill where Adam was buried and the very spot where Christ was crucified. See Jung, *Mysterium Coniunctionis* 388-89. *Planet of the Body; Self-Similar*

orbifold: a higher-dimensional version of a cone. See Kaku, *Hyperspace* 205: "In string theory, our four-dimensional universe may have a six-dimensional twin, which has the topology of an orbifold. However, the six-dimensional universe [background space] is so small that it is unobservable." *Orbifold; Self-Similar*

orbweb like a sink: the gossamer network of the Milky Way compared to a spider's (here, an orb-weaver's) hub of silk. *Heuristic*

orphan: in the poem of the same name, not only Christ extolled as the *lapis*, the philosopher's stone—figuratively, both "the prima materia" (the arcane substance) and "the end-product of the alchemical opus" (Jung, *Mysterium Coniunctionis* 17, 42n2)—but also, literally, an evolving humanoid robot, in the (Slavic) root sense of the latter word, *orb-*, i.e., *separated from his group* like a child without parents. See, in addition, Matt. 8.20: "'the Son of Man has nowhere to lay his head,'" and John 14.18: "'I will not leave you bereft [. . .].'" *Orphan*

orphan smoke: stray fumes that waft from either the tubes of an alchemical retort or the pipes of an industrial factory. *Window*

orphan that grifts: either an embedded cyborg or a humanoid robot that, being a merely technical artifact, swindles and deceives. *Hieroglyph*

Ouroboros: the snake that bites its own tail—a self-described circle—as a symbol of totality. *Arecibo's Dish; Here Be Dragons; Hybrid; Orbifold; Quintessence*

Ouroboros' planet: not only the revolving globe of Earth compared to "the self-devouring dragon that [. . .] begot and gave birth to itself," a symbol of alchemical transformation (Jung, *Alchemical Studies* 259), but also the peregrine speaker likened to one of Christ's "living stones" and built into "a spiritual temple for the holy work of priesthood" (1 Pet. 2.5). *Arecibo's Dish*

ovum: here, the mythological world-egg as well as the human female sex cell. See the photographs of a "traveling" *ovum* in Kitzinger and Nilsson, *Being Born* 11, 13. *Rebis*

Owl in the desert: Cf. Ps. 102: "I am like a desert-owl in the wilderness, / an owl that lives among ruins." *Hybrid*

paintbrush whiskers: electronic sensate "skin" patches tiered like clumps of *paintbrush* bristles—e.g., within Tribble, a test bed for distributed sensing and actuation. *Earthshine*

parallel Flatland shorn: a two-dimensional version of Spacetime stripped of its primordial symmetry and companioned by our three-dimensional world. The name of the Big Bang's ghostly remnant derives from *Flatland: A Romance of Many Dimensions*, a novella written and illustrated by Edwin Abbott Abbot and published in 1884. *The Cheshire of Sense*

Parameter sequence and sensor fed, / By episodes partitioned are we bred: a reference to a recent NASA experiment in which "sensory inputs and motor control parameters were recorded as time-series" and then "used to control" the robotic astronaut (Robonaut) "without the teleoperator" (2806). In effect, the test results showed that "a few teleoperated trials [. . .] of a task are sufficient for enacting a canonical representation of the task" (2811). See Richard Alan Peters II, Christina L. Campbell, William J. Bluethmann, and Eric Huber, "Robonaut Task Learning through Teleoperation," *Proceedings of the 2003 IEEE International Conference on Robotics and Automation*, 14-19 September 2003:2806-11, Vanderbilt University, 13 July 2007<http://www.vuse.vanderbilt.edu/~rap2/papers/ICRA03-Peters-Proc-2806.pdf>. *Canonical*

particulate or crumb: a very minute particle of the Eucharistic Host. In *Psychology and Western Religion*, trans. R. F. C. Hull (Princeton: Princeton UP, 1984), C. G. Jung notes that, at the Holy Sacrifice of the Mass, after the Host is split in two over the chalice, a "small piece, the *particula*, is broken off from the left half [. . .]. The sign of the cross is made over the chalice with the *particula*, and then the priest drops it into the wine" (115). In effect, "the body, or *particula*, is steeped in wine, symbolizing spirit, and this amounts to a glorification of the body. Hence the justification for regarding the *commixtio* [the mingling of the bread and wine] as a symbol of the resurrection" (116). *The Foliate Pebble*

peacock: "an early Christian symbol for the Redeemer" (Jung, *Psychology and Alchemy* 419), since its "combination of all colors" signifies wholeness (223). *Mindlinks; The Robot Not Yet Human*

Peer-to-peer his ambit: an allusion not only to the distributed, local control of Robonaut's sensate skin "cells," but also to the re-defined "master/slave" relationship achieved by the dexterous android and his human operator. *Earthshine*

pelican: either the large, web-footed bird with a long, straight bill that feeds its young with its own blood (a symbol of the salvific Christ) or—because of its resemblance to the *pelican*—an alchemical retort, the philosophical vessel also called, along with the goose and the stork, "the bird of Hermes [Trismegistus]." See Jung, *Psychology and Alchemy* 370n79. *Heuristic*

a perfect eight: a numerical symbol that, as "a multiple of four," represents psychological wholeness (Jung, *Aion* 224). *Self-Assembled*

perilune: the point nearest to the center of the moon in the orbit of a spacecraft. *Rebis*

Philosophy quartered: an allusion to "the squaring of the circle, [. . .] a symbol of the *opus alchymicum*," the latter process conceived by the adepts as the redemption of matter, "since it breaks down the original chaotic unity into the four elements and then combines them again in a higher [spiritual] unity" (Jung, *Psychology and Alchemy* 124). *Mindlinks*

Phoebe: in Greek mythology, one of two sisters whom the twins Castor and Pollux abducted and married. After jealous suitors killed Castor, he shared the gift of immortality that Zeus had already bestowed upon his brother. *On the Care and Feeding of Robots*

photon: an elementary particle; a quantum or packet of light. *Holons; Orphan; Transconscious*

pinwheel: the Milky Way Galaxy, with its vast spiral wheel of stars. *Arecibo's Dish*

Pinwheel astronaut: an astronaut likened simultaneously to a revolving fireworks wheel of colored light, to a pinworm that appears to bite its own tail, and to a human foetus that also forms a spiral shape. However, the signal image evoked is that of a stellar pinwheel, "the long, curving dust tail" of a star, the "ghostly" sight described by John Noble Wilford in "Peering Through Dust at a Stellar Pinwheel," *New York Times* 13 Apr. 1999, New England ed.: D4. Observing the "spiral pattern of the dust streaming 18 billion miles out from the star Wolf-Rayet 104," Wilford writes that "It looked as if a cosmic typewriter had left a fat, upside-down comma hanging out there in the direction of the constellation Sagittarius." *The Foliate Pebble*

Pisces' reign: an allusion to the astrological sign that augurs the coming of Christ's kingdom. See Jung, *Aion* 90. *A Single Day*

The Platonic Man: an "archetypal concept of a perfect being [. . .] round on all sides and uniting within himself the two sexes" (Jung, *Alchemical Studies* 26). *The Platonic Man*

Pneumatic his skills: Pressurized air muscles enable the robot to execute his tasks. *The Atom of the Word*

point: "the symbol of a mysterious creative centre in nature," i.e., the indivisible body of the Godhead (Jung, *Mysterium Coniunctionis* 44-45). *Cadmus and the Sown Men of Thebes; The Cheshire of Sense; Here Be Dragons; The Novenary Foetus; The Platonic Man; Rebis; Reuben's Mandrakes; Self-Similar; Seminal; A Single Day*

premises unknown: a pun—a house and its physical location, as well as the major and minor propositions in a deductive argument. *Arecibo's Dish*

Primer of reference: in Genetics, a segment of nucleic acid needed to initiate DNA replication. *Holons*

Programmed hierophant, the One that we know: Jesus arrived on Earth not only as the Savior and Great High Priest that we recognize "through faith and the Holy Spirit" (Murray, *The Spirit of Christ* 149), but also, like us, as the carrier of a standard genetic code. *Eve's Microchip*

Progresses with eyes on both of his sides: In philosophical alchemy, the first Adam evolves—like Mercurius, "the 'twin' made of 'two natures'" (Jung, *Alchemical Studies* 217)—either as a winged and wingless dragon (a pneumatic and corporeal being) or as a two-headed crowned hermaphrodite. *A Single Day*

pulse of glory: Cf. the paradisal vision described by the English mystic Edward

Maitland (AD 1824-97), in Jung, *Alchemical Studies* 26-27: "I succeeded in polarizing the whole of the convergent rays of my consciousness into the desired focus. And at the same time, as if through the sudden ignition of the rays thus fused into a unity, I found myself confronted with a glory of unspeakable whiteness and of a luster so intense as well-nigh to beat me back. [...] It was the dual form of the Son . . . the unmanifest made manifest, the unformulated formulate, the unindividuate individuate, God as the Lord, proving through His duality that God is Substance as well as Force, Love as well as Will, Feminine as well as Masculine, Mother as well as Father." *Pulse of Glory*

Punctum: in Gnostic texts, the indivisible point (here, a spark of light) construed as an "objective" symbol of the self. See Jung, *Aion* 218-21. *Grainy Abstract Plenum*

Pushpin: a computing system for clusters of sensor nodes that "have the form factor of a *Pushpin* [i.e., a map pin or a thumb tack] that can be inserted anywhere into a large planar substrate, from which they draw their power" (34). See J. A. Paradiso, J. Lifton, and M. Broxton, "Sensate media—multimodal electronic skins as dense sensor networks," *BT Technology Journal* 22.4 [2004]: 32-44, *MIT Media* 12 Oct. 2005 <http://www.media.mit.edu/resenv/pubs/papers/2004-10-BTJJ.pdf>. *Earthshine*

quark: any of a group of six subatomic particles, plus their anti-particles. Quarks are "heavy and strongly interacting, and make up nuclear matter" (Paul Davies, *The Mind of God* [New York: Simon, 1992] 210). *Dancing in the Dark*

Quaternity's cone: a single light *cone*—in the mind of the speaker, a sutured hourglass not unlike the shape of the human percipient and hence an image of the total self, a psychologically quadratic figure (Jung, *Aion* 224). This section of the poem also contains a hidden conceit: the squaring of the circle, an apt symbol of the alchemical *opus*, since the latter process "breaks down the original chaotic unity into the four elements and then combines them in a higher unity. Unity is represented by a circle and the four elements by a square." In other words, "The spirit (or spirit and soul) is the *ternarius* or number three which must first be separated from the body [the fourth] and, after the purification of the latter, infused back into it" (Jung, *Psychology and Alchemy* 124-25). *Arecibo's Dish*

Quaternity's rink: a region in Spacetime compared to the smooth surface of a rectangular floor of ice suitable for skating, hockey, and curling. *Orbifold*

quintessence: not only an alchemical name for the ancient and medieval concept of the aether, a pure fifth element after earth, fire, water, and air—symbolically, "the ever-hoped-for and never-to-be-discovered 'One'" (Jung, *Psychology and Alchemy* 124), but also, in modern physics, a theoretical form of dark energy invoked to explain the accelerating universe. *Quintessence*

qwiffs: quantum wave functions that describe "the probability of an observation and not the actual observation" (Fred Alan Wolf, *Taking the Quantum Leap* [New York: Harper, 1981] 170). An offshoot of wave-particle duality, "They are called functions because they are functional, which means [that] they depend on things for their operation"—on space and time (186). In effect, "Qwiffs represent what *could* take place in reality." Nevertheless, as ghostly, quantum-jumping particles, "Qwiffs predict *with uncertainty* [emphasis added] the behavior of matter" (219). *Grainy Abstract Plenum; Hieroglyph; Hybrid*

rapt: either seized by God or engrossed in meditation. *The Atom of the Word*

ream: here, a large quantity of inspired testamental matter. *The Autonomous Android*

Rebis: an androgyne, the "dual being born of the alchemical union of opposites" (masculine/feminine) and recognized "as a symbol of the self" (Jung, *Aion* 268). The word is pronounced RAY-bis. *The Atom of the Word; Cadmus and the Sown Men of Thebes; Canonical; Dancing in the Dark; Earthshine; Eve's Microchip; Heart of Flesh; Hybrid; The Lantern with Two Lights; Mindlinks; The Novenary Foetus; Orphan; Planet of the Body; The Platonic Man; Rebis; Reuben's Mandrakes; The Robot Not Yet Human; Screen; Self-Assembled; Seminal; A Single Day; Son of One Day; Sunship; Tattoo; When I Was a Foetus; Window*

red Damascene earth: in Cabalistic literature, the soil from which the first Adam was created (Jung, *Alchemical Studies* 318). *Damascene* is the adjectival form of Damascus, widely regarded as the oldest *continuously* inhabited city in the world. *The Platonic Man*

reeled out past her: Apparently the speaker became, like Christ, a "fisher of men" (Matt. 4.19) even as he crisscrossed Maya's web—"the illusory world of the senses"—beyond its deadly hub. See Jung, *Psychology and Alchemy* 217, fig. 108, and also 77, fig. 28, where Christ captures the Leviathan "with the sevenfold tackle of the line of David" and "with the crucifix as bait." *The Foliate Pebble*

The regimen of Mars: one in a series of alchemical procedures that represent cyclical death and renewal. Thus, at the end of the regimen of Venus, "the colour changes into a livid purple, whereupon the philosophical tree will blossom. Then follows the regimen of Mars [. . .]," during which the soaring colors of the rainbow and of the peacock appear (Jung, *Mysterium Coniunctionis* 288-89). *Eve's Microchip; Orbifold*

REMs that sigh: here, both the shorthand for the rapid eye movements of dreamers who grieve or murmur in their sleep and a synecdoche for the dreamers themselves. *Reuben's Mandrakes*

Resin of the wise *concealed in the drum*: "a synonym for the transforming substance," the life force likened by the alchemists "to the 'glue of the world,'" a red gum [originally gum arabic] fixed as "the medium between mind and body and the union of both" (Jung, *Psychology and Alchemy* 161). Here, the *drum* is Gaea's belly. *The Foliate Pebble*

Resonant string: According to *string* theory, instead of a "laundry list of particle species, [. . .] there is only *one* fundamental ingredient—the string—and the wealth of particle species simply reflects the different vibrational patterns that a string can execute" (Brian Greene, *The Fabric of the Cosmos* [New York: Knopf, 2004] 346). *Dancing in the Dark*

Reuben's mandrakes: a Biblical image that connotes both procreative power and carnal pleasure. After Rachel permitted Leah to sleep with their husband Jacob in exchange for *mandrakes* (magical plants that increased fertility and that Leah had been given by Reuben, her firstborn son), Leah "conceived and bore a fifth son" (Gen. 30.16-17). *Reuben's Mandrakes*

ribboned aster: Christ's latterday "astral" coheir—the "Citizen of the Cosmos"—modified by his intertwined strands of DNA. In *Alchemical Studies*, Jung affirms that, for Paracelsus, "'The true man is the star [i.e., the heavenly light] in us'" (131). *The Foliate Pebble*

the ride in the wain: an embellishment of the scene in John 18.12-24. Here, the addition is the *wain* or wagon that "shuttled" Christ between the houses of two High Priests—Annas and Caiaphas—and that led Him, as a result, to "harrowing" crucifixion and "abhorrent" death. See Ian Wilson, *Jesus: The Evidence* (Washington, D. C.: Regnery, 2000) 125-34. *Earthshine*

rind: the outer skin of the papyrus plant, *Cyperus papyrus*, from which ancient Egyptian scrolls were made. *When I Was a Foetus*

Rivers of water, belly that we plumb: in Gnostic symbolism, paradisal waters that pour into the world through the four gospels and that flow from "the belly of Christ" (Jung, *Aion* 215). Cf. John 7.37-38: "Jesus stood and cried aloud, 'If anyone is thirsty let him come to me; whoever believes in me, let him drink.'" *The Foliate Pebble*

Robonaut: NASA's robotic astronaut, a "state-of-the-art humanoid" designed for space travel. "Outside the spacecraft, it will perform its tasks under the control of a human operator at a tele-presence console" (Menzel and D'Aluisio, *Robo sapiens* 129). *Canonical; Leprous; Robonaut; Self-Similar; Silverfoot; Spiritual Laws*

The Rock of Horeb: Cf. Exod. 17.6, where the Israelites drink a supernatural water that pours out of "a rock in Horeb," the latter a prefiguration of the *Rock* that is Christ. See also 1 Cor. 10.3-4. *On the Care and Feeding of Robots*

Root of itself: For the alchemists, the *prima materia* was—among its many symbolical names—"the One and the root of itself" (Jung, *Alchemical Studies* 139). See, for example, "Physica Trithemii" (*Theatrum chemicum*, vol. 1 [Strasbourg, 1659]) 391, where Gerhard Dorn declares that the One "is simple and consists of the number four" and, further, that this [the quaternity as designated unity] "is the centre of the natural wisdom, whose circumference, closed in itself, forms a circle: an immeasurable order reaching to infinity" (qtd. in Jung, *Alchemical Studies* 150-51). *The Foliate Pebble*

Rotund alembic: in alchemy, the round upper part—the capital or still-head—of a two-part distillation apparatus. *The Cheshire of Sense*

***rotundum*:** in alchemy, the "round, original form" of "the spiritual, inner and complete man" (C. G. Jung, *Mandala Symbolism*, trans. R. F. C. Hull [1959; Princeton: Princeton UP, 1973] 9-10). *Rebis*

Routed to a portal tiled like a tin: The speaker refers not only to the android, the "Bipedal twin" diverted to his workstation on a space shuttle, but also to the ultradense electronic skin patches *tiled* over, or embedded in, the body of the dexterous robot, "with every signal from the patches routed [or wired out] to multiplexing arrays [or groups of data] and a central digital processor." See Paradiso et al., "Sensate media—multimodal electronic skins as dense sensor networks," *BT Technology Journal* 32. *Earthshine*

Rubato: an Italian word meaning *stolen* time; hence, in Music, a relaxation of tempo. *Template*

Rub away the pupil, beam not splinter: an ironic variation on Matt. 7.4-5: "how can you say to your brother, 'let me take the speck out of your eye,' when all the time there is that plank in your own? You hypocrite! First take the plank out of your own eye, and then you will see clearly to take the speck out of your brother's." Here, of course, the *pupil* refers not only to the black, contractile opening in the center of the iris, but also to the blemished "sprinter" of line 15, the Christian disciple himself. *Cinderdust*

runner at the start: Cf. 1 Cor. 9.24: "You know (do you not?) that at the sports all the runners run the race, though only one wins the prize. Like them, run to win!" *Son of One Day*

salamander's coal: In *Mysterium Coniunctionis*, Jung identifies the salamander as "the Mercurial serpent [. . .] whom the fire does not consume [. . .]" and who apparently signifies the alchemical process of calcination (441). However, according to Charbonneau-Lassay, "Chastity and virginity also claim the salamander as emblem," since these virtues "pass through the midst of the passions flaming around them without being burned" (*The Bestiary of Christ* 177). In addition, the Middle Ages had made this frolicking, morally ambivalent reptile "the image of Christ because of his kingship over fire" (178-79). *Orphan*

salted with the salt of wisdom: Cf. not only Jung, *Mysterium Coniunctionis* 246, where the German alchemist Johann Rudolf Glauber (AD 1604-1670) "says that his favorite disciple John was 'salted with the salt of wisdom,'" but also Mark 9.49 (AV), where the Messiah promises that "every one shall be salted with fire, and every sacrifice shall be salted with salt" (239). *The Autonomous Android*

salt in the vas: "the arcane substance" in the Hermetic vessel. For the alchemists, "Christ is the salt of wisdom which is given at baptism" (Jung, *Mysterium Coniunctionis* 241). *The Atom of the Word*

Saturn yet astray: "The rings [of *Saturn*] face the earth every 15 years, alternately showing the northern and the southern hemisphere. When the rings are seen edge-on, they disappear, indicating thickness of merely a few miles" (Sune Engelbrektson, *Stars, Planets, and Galaxies* [New York: Bantam, 1975] 104). *A Single Day*

scabbards: sheaths that encase swords or daggers. *A Single Day*

Scarabs of insight: unicorned sun-beetles. In *The Bestiary of Christ*, Charbonneau-Lassay describes the scarab as "the emblem of the swift, vivifying, and intelligent ray of the sun, the *spiritus et mens*, *logos* or *ratio* of the Ancients, that is, the breath of life, the soul, the understanding, the inspired word, reason" (335). *The Novenary Foetus*

scars in the gland: wound-repair or healing tissue in the testis, one of the two male generative glands; hence, a hidden reference to the Gnostic first Adam as a semi-castrated androgyne. *Hieroglyph*

scintilla: in medieval alchemy, the soul-spark that reflects God's descent into matter. *Churning-Stick; Orphan*

scroll of the tun: rolled ornamental work that adorns a large cask—here, of wine. *Transconscious*

sealed like a bird: Cf. the picture of the peacock "rising [like Christ] from the [alchemical] retort" (Jung, *Psychology and Alchemy* 418). *The Atom of the Word*

A seal like a stone inscribed with a name: Cf. Rev. 2.17: "'Hear, you who have ears to hear, what the Spirit says to the churches! To him who is victorious I will give some of the hidden manna; I will give him also a white stone, and on the stone will be written a new name, known to none but him that receives it.'" *Robonaut*

Seamless as the sexes: Cf. Gal. 3.28: "There is no such thing as Jew and Greek, slave and freeman, male and female; for you are all one person in Christ Jesus." *Arecibo's Dish*

Secure its vise: The creators of the metal man fasten its body to a tendril-like workbench device used for holding an object being worked on. Cf. Menzel and D'Aluisio, *Robo sapiens* 130, where an "experimental, high-tech" droid is "bolted to the ceiling" of its makers' lab. *Leprous*

Seed in the silicon: the Christian Savior compared to a robot encoded in a microchip and implanted in Gaea's womb. *Canonical*

Selene crescive: in Greek mythology, a moon-goddess, here related to the black Shulamite of The Song of Songs 6.13, as well as to the sun-woman of Rev. 12.1 (Jung, *Mysterium Coniunctionis* 433-34). *A Single Day*

Self-born enigma: the *total* conscious and unconscious individual "shrouded in 'metaphysical' darkness" (Jung, *Psychology and Alchemy* 182)—a cosmic riddle without beginning or ending. *Arecibo's Dish*

self-sown: self-fertilized, i.e., spiritually renewed. *The Atom of the Word; The Foliate Pebble; Hybrid*

senses, feels, discerns, / Intuits the cosmos: According to Jung, "The orienting system of consciousness has four aspects, which correspond to four empirical functions: thinking, feeling, sensation (sense-perception), [and] intuition," an "archetypal arrangement" that "always expresses a totality" (*Alchemical Studies* 167). *Self-Assembled*

Serpentine hieroglyph: another Hermetic symbol of wholeness—the mercurial dragon that "impregnates, begets, bears, devours, and slays himself" (Jung, *Alchemical Studies* 223). *Hieroglyph*

shadow like the Goth: the inky darkness that pervades the cosmos, as well as the proclivity to evil that contaminates human nature. *Citizen of the Cosmos*

Shadow matter: clumps and halos of dark—i.e., invisible—*matter* that fill the universe. *The Cheshire of Sense*

shaman: either a priest or a magus or a holy man with supernatural powers. *Robonaut*

Sheba: the Queen of *Sheba*, who visited King Solomon in order "to test him with hard questions" and to experience his reputed wisdom (1 Kings 10.1-13). *Dancing in the Dark*

Shell like a nautilus; [. . .] / Crescent self-sown: Through circular—even serpentine images—the speaker, a child of the sun as well as of the moon, identifies himself as both coheir of Christ and crowned hermaphrodite. The image of the Ouroboros ("the dragon who marries himself") as a symbol of self-origination and that of the healing serpent of Moses as a precursor of the crucified Christ also figure here. See Jung, *Mysterium Coniunctionis* 293n138. *The Foliate Pebble*

Sheol: In *Handbook to the Gospels* (Ann Arbor: Servant, 1979), John Wijngaards helpfully discriminates between the hell of the eternally damned and *Sheol*, "'the place of the dead,' the home (in Jewish theology) of all the dead [...]. When we say that Jesus descended into hell we mean only (in the terminology of the Bible) that he was truly dead; he was no longer in the 'land of the living' but went down into the 'land of the dead'" (244-45), as every human sojourner must. *The Foliate Pebble; Spiritual Laws*

She stows its trace: Gaea, the goddess of the Earth, conceals faint suggestions no less than mirrored images of wave-particle duality. In other words, as Arthur Zajonc demonstrates in *Catching the Light*, since "One thing—the photon—seems somehow simultaneously related to two distinct paths," it may well be that, "for light, at least, the most fundamental feature is not to be found in smallness, but rather in wholeness, [in] its incorrigible capacity to be one and many, [real] particle and [probabilistic] wave, a single thing with the universe inside" (299). *Arecibo's Dish*

shield and buckler: symbols of the martial "characters" or attributes that the sixteenth-century alchemist Gerhard Dorn assigned to Venus because "love overcomes all obstacles" (qtd. in Jung, *Alchemical Studies* 175). *Seminal*

Shulamite's moonlight: In The Song of Songs 6.13, the *Shulamite* is the woman from Shulem or ancient Shunem who represents—for the alchemists—the "dark, feminine [lunar] form" (an essential component) of the totalistic self (Jung, *Mysterium Coniunctionis* 157). *Dancing in the Dark*

shuttlewalk His beat: Attached to their jet-propelled backpacks, NASA's shuttle astronauts patrol Jesus' *beat*, their assigned route in low-Earth orbit. The transitive verb, a neologism, suggests a cheerful form of (cosmic) police authority, as in the English-language idiom "walk his beat." *Tattoo*

Sidewinder's sign: a variant image of the Ouroboros, both "tail-eating serpent" (Jung, *Psychology and Alchemy* 345) and alchemical symbol of wholeness. *Sunship*

Sighted eye, the entryway to a beam / Still hooked on night: a tangled syzygy, or pair of opposites. The human *eye* that "entwines" the light is *hooked on* (both fastened to and obsessed with) primordial darkness (Zajonc, *Catching the Light* 2). *Arecibo's Dish*

Sight's saffron carapace: the shiny, orange-yellow, "high-strength, aluminum alloy endoskeleton" of the NASA Robonaut, who becomes, in this poem, a chthonic archetype of the Christian Savior activated by His prescient coheir. See "Robonaut Materials," *Robonaut*, NASA, 20 June 2007 <http://robonaut.jsc.nasa.gov/materials.htm>. *Leprous*

Siloam's flow: in John 9.1-7, waters from the Pool of Siloam, where Jesus cured a blind man. *Mindlinks*

Silver elixir: a lunar symbol; in alchemical texts, the spiritual water "which wakens the dead sleeping in Hades to a new springtime" (Jung, *Alchemical Studies* 78). *Self-Similar*

Silverfoot: NASA's uniped Robonaut, a humanoid designed for space travel. *Leprous; Silverfoot*

a single day: Cf. Jung, *Alchemical Studies* 79n64: Ouroboros, the self-devouring, self-fertilizing dragon, "brings itself forth in a single day." *A Single Day*

Sion: here, both Zion, "that new Jerusalem" proclaimed by "the Son of God" (Rev. 3.12), and scion, a descendant or an offspring. *Rebis*

slake: a pun. In its transitive form, the verb *slake* means either to quench [a thirst] or to satisfy [a desire]; in its intransitive form, it means to disintegrate—here, like rusted iron robots that crumble from exposure to the air. *The Novenary Foetus*

solid white snow: In sundry Hermetic tracts, the mercurial Spirit of the Lord "flies [purified] like solid white snow" (Jung, *Alchemical Studies* 214). *A Single Day*

Some astrum with fingers: according to Paracelsus, the star—the primordial "man of light"—that "clothed himself in Adam's body" and that exists within each of us (*Alchemical Studies* 131n52, 137). *When I Was a Foetus*

Some doors open from the inside, *Castor*: a final clause—the speaker's self-directed apostrophe—that superimposes images of copulation, birth, and affectivity. Cf. Thomas Bezansen, "Endpoint," *IONS Noetic Sciences Review* 2 (1999): 64: "Some doors open only from the inside." Here, the crucial addition is *Castor* (the twin brother of Pollux), a hyphenated Everyman belonging both to Heaven and to Earth. *The Foliate Pebble*

Son of one day: in John 1.5, "the Light, the Logos" of the first *day* of Creation "who is [also] the Johannine Christ" (Jung, *Mysterium Coniunctionis* 338). *Son of One Day*

Son of the Son: the individual percipient reborn through Christ. In other words, like a father, the Savior teaches the speaker how to be a son. Cf. Eph. 1.5: "he [Yahweh] destined us [. . .] to be accepted as his sons through Jesus Christ." *Tattoo*

So, Typhon pursuing him, Pisces shunts / In the wettest place that the foetus fronts: In Greek mythology, Typhon, the monster with a hundred dragon heads, had pursued Leto when her son Apollo "was still in her womb; but she fled to the floating island of Delos on a 'night sea journey' and was there safely delivered of her child" (Jung, *Symbols of Transformation* 371). Here, of course, *Pisces*, who *shunts* or turns aside in order to conquer the serpent, represents not only Christ, both sun-hero and "Goat-Fish," but also His womb-entwining coheir, the speaker himself. In other words, the latterday galactic pilgrim, being reborn, has just emerged—like the Son of God—from "'the wettest place on earth,' [. . .] the maternal depths" (198). *Rebis*

Soul-spark: in Cabalistic texts, the spirit that descends into matter. *Churning-Stick*

Spacetime, hyphenate, re-collects Her rune: Divided between Spirit and Body, *Spacetime*—here, a metonym for Gaea, the Mother of the Universe—remembers (recollects) even as She gathers (*re-collects*) the substance of Her cosmic riddle. A *rune* is a mystical—and therefore an elusive—song or poem. *Arecibo's Dish*

spagyric: pertaining to an alchemical process that both separates and combines (Jung, *Mysterium Coniunctionis* 481n91). Thus, the *spagyric* foetus ascends into Heaven that it may become a spirit from a body and then descends to earth that it may become a body again. Cf. John 3.13: "No one ever went up into heaven except the one who came down from heaven, the Son of Man whose home is in heaven." *On the Care and Feeding of Robots; The Platonic Man*

sparks and limbs: Cf. Christian Knorr von Rosenroth, *Kabbala Denudata*, vol. 2

(Frankfurt, 1684) 248: "'(He [Ezekiel] says [in Ezek. 34.31], as it were, that all the souls of the Israelists were in truth nothing but the first-created Adam.) And you were his sparks and his limbs'" (qtd. in Jung, *Mysterium Coniunctionis* 413). *The Platonic Man*

sparrows sold for a small coin: Cf. Luke 12.6: "'Are not sparrows five for twopence? And yet not one of them is overlooked by God.'" *Technical Jesus*

spars in the skein: a snapshot of NASA's Hubble Space Telescope repair mission in December 1999—the space shuttle Discovery's metal poles or rigging twined in the net of the cosmic vacuum. See "Long Distance House Call," *Team Hubble Servicing Mission 3A*, 9 Sept. 2006 <http://hubblesite.org/the_telescope/teamhubble/servicing_missions.php>. *Hieroglyph*

Sphere of the Trinity: The Neo-Pythagoreans held that God, as the world-soul, "is a circle or sphere." The round nature of the stone suggests the lunar or feminine aspect of God (Jung, *Psychology and Alchemy* 325). *The Foliate Pebble*

spherule in the gloam: any star perceived as a small sphere or globule embedded in the dusk. *Planet of the Body*

***Spin of a mystic number, boson's* ping**: See Timothy Ferris, *The Whole Shebang: A State-of-the-Universe(s) Report* (New York: Simon, 1997) 220-21: "Subatomic particles can be divided into two classes: those whose spin is fractional (one-half) and those whose spin is an integer (one). Fractional-spin particles are called *fermions*. Integer-spin particles are *bosons*. [. . .] Generally speaking, fermions constitute matter while bosons carry force." *Grainy Abstract Plenum*

spiral arms that swing: Cf. Engelsbrektson, *Stars, Planets, and Galaxies* 124: "What appears from earth as the continuous band of the Milky Way is really [the] three separate spiral arms" of Sagittarius, Orion, and Perseus. *Reuben's Mandrakes*

spouse that he nears / From all nations chosen: "Ge's *technical Jesus*," the post-biological son of Adam, seeks to share the heritage of God's royal priesthood. See not only Matt. 28.19: "'Go forth therefore and make all nations my disciples [. . .],'" but also Eph. 1.4: "In Christ he chose us before the world was founded, to be dedicated, to be without blemish in his sight, to be full of love [. . .]." *Technical Jesus*

spring-point of Pisces, goat or teddy: In *Aion*, Jung suggests that, "to the extent that Christ was regarded as the new aeon, it would be clear to anyone acquainted with astrology that he was born as the first fish of the Pisces era, and was doomed to die as the last ram [or (scape)goat] [. . .] of the declining Aries era. [Thus,] Matt. 27.15ff. hands down this mythologem in the form of the old sacrifice of the seasonal god" (90). Concerning the shifting *spring-point*, Jung calculates that "Astrologically the beginning of the next aeon [. . .] falls between A.D. 2000 and 2200" (94n84). The *teddy* mentioned here is Ursa Minor, or the Lesser Bear, the latter constellation being the home of Polaris, the North Star, as well as the storied co-ruler (with Aquarius) of the approaching age. *Citizen of the Cosmos*

the sprinter: God's athlete, as in Heb. 12.1-2: "And what of ourselves? With all these witnesses to faith around us like a cloud, we must throw off every encumbrance, every sin to which we cling, and run with resolution the race for which we are entered, our eyes fixed on Jesus, on whom faith depends from start to finish [. . .]." *Cinderdust*

stand-still: here, not only the (summer or winter) solstice, when the sun is at its greatest distance from the celestial equator and therefore appears to "stand still," but also a cessation of progress, as in a conflict. *Churning-Stick*

stars in the band: globular clusters that orbit the center of our Galaxy. Cf. Engelbrektson, *Stars, Planets, and Galaxies* 23: "The *Milky Way* appears as a hazy band of light from millions of stars." *Hieroglyph*

statolith: an otolith—a stone or calcareous particle found in a vestibular sac in the middle ear. It is not only sensitive to gravity, but also indicative of linear position when the subject moves. *Technical Jesus*

Still a man and a woman embracing: "the androgynous original man or Anthropos of Gnosticism [. . .], whose parallel in India is *purusha*. Of him the Brihad-aranyaka Upanishad says: 'He was as large as a man and woman embracing. He divided his self [Atman] in two, and thence arose husband and wife. He united himself with her and men were born' [. . .]. The common origin of these ideas lies in the primitive notion of the bisexual original man" (Jung, *Psychology and Alchemy* 161-62). *Sunship*

Still with apples of the Spirit bowed down: the immortal fruit of the philosophical tree, the latter a symbol of the alchemical *opus*. The fruit itself represents the higher spiritual being baptized into Christ. See *Alchemical Studies* 51-52 and also 309n11, where Jung quotes from the hymn for St. Paul of Constantinople in Theodore the Studite (AD 759-826): "'O most blessed one, from the cradle thou didst flourish like a comely plant in the ascetic garden; thou gavest forth a pleasant odour, bowed down with the finest apples of the Holy Spirit.'" *Cadmus and the Sown Men of Thebes*

string: In *The Whole Shebang*, Timothy Ferris indicates that, according to superstring theories, "subatomic particles are actually tiny strings made of space. [. . .] Strings are so small that when viewed from a distance—meaning at any wavelength of light or any other form of electromagnetic illumination—they 'look like' infinitesimal particles" (220). *Reuben's Mandrakes*

Strings of ones and zeros: the output of a program used in an electronic computer. *Arecibo's Dish*

Subcutaneous: under the skin—hence, infelt. *The Autonomous Android*

Submersed all his souls: In Cabalistic writings, God has hidden *all* the *souls* in the aqueous body of the Primordial Man, who contains everything and "is himself the world" (Jung, *Mysterium Coniunctionis* 413n198). *Silverfoot*

subset: Earth viewed as a data structure, a portion of a mathematical set. *Arecibo's Dish*

such a City as nomads raze: "the holy city, new Jerusalem" (Rev. 21.2), to which the "wealth and splendour of the nations shall be brought" (Rev. 21.26) and which restless cultural wanderers seek to demolish. *Cadmus and the Sown Men of Thebes*

Such souls as exist have out of him rained: Cf. Jung, *Mysterium Coniunctionis* 413-14: For the Cabalists, the first-created Adam "appears on the one hand as the body of the people of Israel and on the other as its 'general soul.' [. . .] As the inner man, however, he is the totality of the individual, the synthesis of all parts of the psyche, and therefore of the conscious and the unconscious." Thus, from a Jungian perspective, "The 'going out' of the souls from the Primordial Man can be understood as the projection of a psychic integration process: the saving wholeness of the inner man—i.e., the 'Messiah'—cannot come about until all parts of the psyche have been made conscious." *The Platonic Man*

Sundered from all secondness: Meister Eckhart (AD 1260?-1327?) defines the mystic seeker's exemplary union with God in *Works*, trans. C. de B. Evans, vol. 1 (London, 1924) 247-48: "Love him as he is: a not-spirit, a not-person, a not-image; as a sheer, pure, clear One, which he is, sundered from all secondness; and in this One let us sink eternally, from nothing to nothing. So help us God. Amen" (qtd. in Jung, *Aion* 193). *Cinderdust; Orbifold*

supercluster's brace: the Perseus-Pisces complex of galaxies, the latter a chain of clusters that links the selfsame *brace* or pair of constellations and that occurs along the plane of the Milky Way. *Planet of the Body*

The supplemental cosmos: the mere trace of Spacetime—an added-on, "*in-the-place-of-itself*" world that "*we no longer know*," because "we are beyond absolute knowledge" and because "the thing itself always escapes" (Jacques Derrida, *Speech and Phenomena and Other Essays on Husserl's Theory of Signs*, trans. David B. Allison [Evanston: Northwestern UP, 1973] 89, 103-04). *Screen*

Surveils the Chalice: After pronouncing the words of Consecration, the metallic hierophant genuflects; adores the Precious Blood; rises; and then elevates, even as he surveils or watches, the Eucharistic *Chalice*. See *Saint Joseph Daily Missal* (1959; New York: Catholic Book, 1961) 678. *The Atom of the Word*

swing or steady: two theories that posit the origin of the universe and that Paul Davies explains in *The Mind of God*: oscillating, in which "the universe varies as it expands and contracts in a cyclic manner" (52), and steady-state, in which the universe has neither beginning nor end because "the average density of matter [. . .] remains unchanged"—in other words, the law of conservation of energy is (supposedly) not violated since "the positive energy of the created matter" is "compensated exactly by the enhanced negative energy of the creation field" (55-56). Davies shows why scientists have rejected both views in favor of an inflationary model in which "a little bubble of space-time [. . .] 'inflated' at a fantastic rate to produce a big bang" (70). See also Ferris, *The Whole Shebang* 229-44. *Citizen of the Cosmos*

Synonymous His bride: Christ and His tabernacled coheirs revealed as One Body. *Citizen of the Cosmos*

Synthesizes speech: Through a voice synthesizer, the robotic celebrant mimics human sounds. *The Atom of the Word*

syzygy: paired opposites that represent wholeness—for example, Male and Female, as in the symbol of the hermaphroditic *rebis*, the God-image "compounded of two parts and therefore," according to the medieval alchemists, "frequently [. . .] an amalgam of Sol and Luna" (Jung, *Psychology and Alchemy* 202). *Hieroglyph; The Platonic Man*

Tabula rasa, *bias of the knoll*: the blank or clean slate that the crucified Christ offered at Golgotha to His redeemed followers. *Heuristic*

tagmeme: the smallest grammatical unit—here, a sound or a word—that functions meaningfully in patterned discourse. *Transconscious*

taileater's Nietzsche: the human sojourner as a synonym for the Ouroboros, the snake that bites its own tail. The German thinker Friedrich *Nietzsche* (AD 1844-1900) is cited here as a free spirit "capable of *golden* laughter" (*Beyond Good and Evil: Prelude to a Philosophy of the Future*, trans. Walter Kaufmann [Vintage-Random, 1966] 232). *Dancing in the Dark*

taproot: a main root from which subsidiary branch roots extend and expand. *Grainy Abstract Plenum*

tattoo "I in You"/ *Wheel like a heart*: a cardioid (a wheel shaped like a heart with a rounded tip) ingrained upon the flesh of the speaker and enfolding, inside its disk, a promise of everlasting spiritual love. Cf. John 14.18-20: "'In a little while the world will see me no longer, but you will see me; because I live, you too will live; then you will know that I am in my Father, and you in me and I in you.'" *Tattoo*

tau* or *tee: both "the primitive Egyptian form of the cross: T" (Jung, *Symbols of Transformation* 264n136) and, from the English alphabet, the letter T. In this poem, the word *tau* rhymes with "now." *Churning-Stick*

Teflon: the trademark for a white, waxy, synthetic cloth used in making the outer protective layer of an astronaut's spacesuit. *Heuristic; Technical Jesus*

Teleports the species: Teleportation is the theoretical transfer of matter from one quantum state to another. In *Space-Time and Beyond*, Bob Toben, "in conversation" with the physicists Jack Sarfatti and Fred Wolf, explains that, since "Every action in 'real' time is an indefinite sequence of materializations and dematerializations on the microscopic quantum level," and since the latter phenomena "occur faster than the speed of light and in such great numbers that perception of this action is continual," it is not inconceivable that "Teleportation could result from a giant quantum jump." However, here, the speaker, commuting "from one space-time path to another," dematerializes and then recreates the *species* (either the outward appearance or copy of the entangled Savior) through the imagination of faith rather than through the "coherence" of "all the constituent particles" (156). *Earthshine*

telepresent: a reference to a system of remote robotic control—in effect, a form of virtual presence. Thus, wearing a Helmet Mounted [Stereo] Display (HMD), along with force and tactile feedback gloves, a human teleoperator senses—even as he simulates—the programmed actions of NASA's Robonaut. *Spiritual Laws*

ten-finger span: See "A mathematical theory proposed by Alan Turing in 1952," which explains an evolutionary advantage, i.e., "molecules for creating [ten] embryonic [human] fingers" (*Science Daily* 31 July 2014: 1-4 <www.sciencedaily.com>). *Hybrid*

Terra incognita: a phrase derived from Latin—an "unknown land"; a remote region that has been neither mapped, nor explored, nor documented. *Heart of Flesh*

tesseract: an unravelled four-dimensional hypercube arranged as a three-dimensional cross (Kaku, *Hyperspace* 72). *Cadmus and the Sown Men of Thebes; Earthshine; Mindlinks; On the Care and Feeding of Robots; Self-Similar*

tesserae: small, cubelike tiles of stone or glass closely set in mosaic designs. *Heart of Flesh*

test bed: in Computer Science, either a software program or both hardware and software components devised for testing purposes. *Canonical*

Through worlds like fields: The speaker alludes to the field framework of modern physics—e.g., electromagnetic *fields*, gravitational *fields*, nuclear *fields*, and Higgs *fields*. See Greene, *The Fabric of the Cosmos* 254-63. *Reuben's Mandrakes*

Thumb like a gum: With a phallic quip, the speaker celebrates *gum* arabic—in alchemy, not just "a synonym for the [adhesive] transforming substance," but also an emblem of "the androgynous original man of Gnosticism" (Jung, *Psychology and Alchemy* 161). *Tattoo*

thumblings: creative dwarfs—chthonic "personifications of the hidden forces of nature" (Jung, *The Archetypes and the Collective Unconscious* 158). *Mindlinks; Planet of the Body; Reuben's Mandrakes*

Till, bedded in the set, the ground infolds: our universe postulated as a finite subset of some infinite meta-universe. See *The Future of Man* (1964; New York: Harper, 1969) 263, where Pierre Teilhard de Chardin speculates that "the stuff of the cosmos [. . .] is not only in a state of spatial expansion [. . .]"; rather, "even more significantly, it presents itself to our experience as actuated by a movement of qualitative in-folding (or arrangement, if you prefer) upon itself; and this 'in-folding arrangement' moves in the direction, not of any homogeneous repetition, but of a formidable growth of complexity, increasing with the passage of time and resulting in proteins, cells and living matter of every kind." *Reuben's Mandrakes*

Till mandrakes like spouses lend their perfume: Cf. Song Sol. 7.12-13: "let us go early to the vineyards [...]. There will I give you my love, / when the mandrakes give their perfume, / and all fruits are ready at our door." Here, as in Gen. 30.16-17, the mandrake, a magical plant reputed to increase fertility, connotes both procreative power and carnal pleasure. However, in the canticle quoted above, since "the bridegroom [who] tells of his delight in his bride" is, according to J. Vernon McGee, none other than the prefigured Savior, the image of the mandrake—of *Mandragora officinarum*, with its bowl-shaped yellow-green flowers and its scented orange-red berries—may also evoke "the outgoing of desire from the heart of Christ" to "His people" (that is to say, in the context of "The Robot Not Yet Human," to autonomous androids, metallic cyborgs, and fleshly coheirs alike). See *Thru the Bible with J. Vernon McGee*, vol. 3 (Nashville: Nelson, 1982) 178-79. *The Robot Not Yet Human*

torque: the rotational effect of force on an object. *The Robot Not Yet Human*

torus: the universe pictured as a hyperdoughnut, one of the "strange topologies" that Michio Kaku predicates in *Hyperspace* 94-98. *Canonical; Hybrid; The Novenary Foetus; Orbifold; Quintessence*

transverse of cones: a reference to the weird trajectory of the light cone in curved space-time. According to Einstein's general theory of relativity, past and future light *cones* may intersect—i.e., overlap—at the hypersurface of the present instant, "so that, in principle, it is possible to experience events now that will be an effect of my future resolves and actions" (H. Weyl, *Space-Time-Matter* [New York: Dover, 1952] 274; qtd. in Toben, "in conversation" with Sarfatti and Wolf, *Space-Time and Beyond* 133). *Holons*

treatise of Shem: an astrological almanac attributed to *Shem*, the eldest son of Noah. Its overall deterministic view of the cosmos yet allows for creation by a benevolent deity. *Self-Similar*

Trismegistus' spark: the divine soul-spark sought by Hermes Trismegistus, legendary first alchemist and emblematic magus. *Dancing in the Dark*

troglodytes: brutish, cave-dwelling tribesmen of a prehistoric race. *Template*

troll: a fabulous creature, either dwarf or giant. *Earthshine; Reuben's Mandrakes*

Twice bisect the Host: an allusion to the alchemical squaring of the circle. Here, the tetradic "Host" (Christ) links both "the step-by-step development of the self from an unconscious state to a conscious one" (Jung, *Aion* 264) and the ritual cross in the circle, the latter image reminiscent of the crucifixion and hence "the painful experience of the union of opposites" (Jung, *Mandala Symbolism* 98). *Transconscious*

Twin of two natures: In the Cabalistic view, "Man and his heavenly prototype are 'twins'" (Jung, *Mysterium Coniunctionis* 413n198). *A Single Day*

Twin unipeds: an alchemical depiction of Mercurius duplex, the simultaneously winged and wingless dragon who, epitomizing the god of commerce, travel, cunning, and thievery, doubles as a symbol of psychological unity. Thus, in one illustrated text, as a mirror of Mercurius, "the king on the left has a blue robe and a black foot," and the king on the right "a black robe and a blue foot." See Jung, *Mysterium Coniunctionis* 506-07 and also Pls. 4-7. *Orphan*

Under the aegis of infinite worth: Here, the NASA astronaut, the new "technical Jesus"—whether a unipedal android or a bipedal cyborg—represents a process of creative evolution recollected *forward* and hence eternized. In other words, "the world continues, and it continues because [ever-evolving into the heritage of God's royal priesthood] it is a repetition" (Kierkegaard, *Repetition*, in *Fear and Trembling/Repetition* 133). See also "*Repetition*: Getting the world back," where Edward F. Mooney explains that, for Kierkegaard, "Pursuit of [true] repetition [...] is pursuit of eternity, the answer to a metaphysical, personal, and existential interest. One gets the world, the finite and familiar, back again, repeated, but now under the aegis of infinite value, limitless importance" (*The Cambridge Companion to Kierkegaard*, ed. Alastair Hannay and Gordon D. Marino [1998; Cambridge: Cambridge UP, 1999] 297). *The Robot Not Yet Human*

uniped: not only Robonaut, NASA's one-footed robotic astronaut, but also the alchemical Monocolus, the one-stemmed, semi-castrated, androgynous version of Mercurius. (See Jung, *Mysterium Coniunctionis* 500n135). *Orphan; The Platonic Man; Robonaut; Silverfoot; Spiritual Laws*

unit: the Manned Maneuvering Unit (MMU), a jet backpack that enables an astronaut to fly independently of the shuttle orbiter. *The Atom of the Word; The Robot Not Yet Human*

unit glassed: the MMU (Manned Maneuvering Unit) couched here as a metonym for the helmeted (and hence glass-encased) astronaut. The phrase evokes the image of the "citizen" as a wandering microcosm. See also Jung's assessment of the Monad (the indivisible point), conceived by the Gnostics as an emblem of "perfect Man" (*Aion* 218-19). *Citizen of the Cosmos*

Until the foam unfurls and then a froth: In *Other Worlds* (New York: Simon, 1980), Paul Davies argues that ripples and waves in the fabric of spacetime—what he calls the local gravitation fields—"become so distorted that they break up into foam. The apparently smooth unbroken surface [of spacetime] is really a seething mass of tiny spume and bubbles [...]" (96). *Citizen of the Cosmos*

upraises the bread: At the Communion of the Faithful, having removed the ciborium from the Tabernacle, "the Priest holds up a Sacred Host before the people and says: '[...] Behold the Lamb of God, behold Him Who takes away the sins of the world'" (*Saint Joseph Daily Missal* 692-93). *The Atom of the Word*

Ur-*text in the dome*: the Judeo-Christian Bible construed as an archetypal script encoded in the human brain. *Planet of the Body*

***vas*:** the Hermetic vessel—"a circular instrument, a [well-sealed] phial of spherical shape" (Jung, *Psychology and Alchemy* 146, 236n15). *The Atom of the Word*

***Vega passing, Arcturus like a crust*:** In June, when the sun reaches the solstice, "Arcturus dominates the western sky while Vega [the brightest star of the summer sky] passes overhead" (Engelbrektson, *Stars, Planets, and Galaxies* 42). See also Moore, *Travellers in Space and Time* 92: "Arcturus is a powerful star. Yet on Earth, at a range of 36 light-years, we can detect almost no heat from it." It seems but a *crust*, a piece of ice-cold earth, and nothing more. *The Foliate Pebble*

***Venusian*:** related to Venus, to both the planet nearest Earth and the Roman goddess of Love. *Heart of Flesh*

***verdigris*:** in the alchemical view, greenness that forms like rust on brass, bronze, or copper and "is the metal's sickness" (Jung, *Psychology and Alchemy* 159). *The Atom of the Word; The Platonic Man; Reuben's Mandrakes*

***Void like the adder*:** both the cosmic singularity projected as a serpentine point and the totalistic "symbol of the uroboros, the snake that bites its own tail" (Jung, *Aion* 190). *Citizen of the Cosmos*

***Vulcan's chart*:** In this stanza, the speaker characterizes Vulcan, the Roman god of fire, metals, and metallurgy, as both Hermetic mystagogue and industrial engineer; hence, the *chart* is none other than *Vulcan's* (human-robot) interface safety data sheet. *On the Care and Feeding of Robots*

***water shed*:** Cf. John 19.34: After the death of Jesus on the Cross, "one of the soldiers stabbed his side with a lance, and at once there was a flow of blood and water." The term "watershed" denotes, of course, a critical dividing point or line, as Jung, highlighting the etymology of the German *Wasserscheide* ("watershed") and *Scheide* ("vagina"), recognizes—with a difference—in *Symbols of Transformation*: "Where the roads *cross* and enter into one another, thereby symbolizing the union of opposites, there is the 'mother,' the object and epitome of all union. Where the roads *divide*, where there is parting, separation, splitting, there we find the 'division,' the cleft—the symbol of the mother and at the same time the essence of what the mother means for us, namely cleavage and farewell" (371). See also Jesus' declaration in Mark 3.35: "'Who is my mother? [...] Whoever does the will of God is [...] my mother.'" *Citizen of the Cosmos*

We become a child and a fish at once: Cf. Jung, *Symbols of Transformation* 198: "The fish in dreams occasionally signifies the unborn child, because the child before its birth lives in the water like a fish"; within weeks, during its fetal phase, "becomes child and fish at once"; and, like the astrological Christ, the first fish of the Pisces era, "is therefore a symbol of renewal and rebirth." *Rebis*

Web like the whirlwind: the Milky Way Galaxy viewed as a gigantic spiral wheel or even as the veil of the cosmic illusionist Maya. *Citizen of the Cosmos*

We etch on our spacecraft's aluminum plate [. . .] / Pioneer or freight: an allusion to a message placed aboard the *Pioneer 10* (a spacecraft launched on 3 March 1972, from Cape Kennedy)—a missive "etched on a 6-inch gold-anodized aluminum plate, [the latter] attached to the antenna support struts of *Pioneer 10*," and—as Carl Sagan asserts in *The Cosmic Connection*—intended "to communicate the locale, epoch, and something of the [benevolent] nature of the builders of the spacecraft" (18-19). Not surprisingly, "The human beings [depicted] are the most mysterious part of the message" (20). *Self-Assembled*

We roll the ball as into a sinter: Fantasizing, we move or turn the cosmic fireball, over and over, playfully, in the palm of the hand, even as we might shift a still-burning coal. *Cinderdust*

Westar: i.e., *Westar VI*, an errant geosynchronous communications satellite that shuttle astronauts (Dale Gardner and Joseph Allen) "plucked" from orbit and returned to Earth on 16 November 1984 (Kerrod, *Space Walks* 46). *Himalayan*

When the robot rotates, protect his arm; / Do not dangle his bulk: In "Robot care and feeding," Tom Horton and Aravind Srinivasan remind each designated human operator that one must not only "avoid picking up the [shared] robot in a way that would cause its bulk to dangle from a connector [. . .]," but also "take care not to smash the gripper arm into anything when commanding the robot to turn or rotate" (*CS 340*, 25 Jan. 2007, U of Virginia, Charlottesville, 2 May 2007 <http.//www.virginia.edu/~cs340/robot-care-and-feeding/index.html>). *On the Care and Feeding of Robots*

White foliated earth: foliated (or layered) white earth (*terra alba foliata*), i.e., the brain; the marrow or "inwards of the head" framed as "a synonym for the arcane substance," the primordial stuff of life. Alchemically, the brain is "the abode of the divine part" (Jung, *Mysterium Coniunctionis* 435). *Arecibo's Dish*

White stone *by Yahweh signed*: See Rev. 2.17: "'Hear, you who have ears to hear, what the Spirit says to the churches! To him who is victorious I will give some of the hidden manna; I will give him also a white stone, and on the stone will be written a new name, known to none but him that receives it.'" *When I Was a Foetus*

"Why should this happen to me?" *asks the sage*: Cf. Jung, *Psychology and Alchemy* 117: "The wise man [. . .] will ask himself: Who am I that all this should happen to me? To find the answer to this fateful question he will look into his own heart." *Churning-Stick*

The widow of Nain (NAY-in): In Luke 7.11-17, Jesus journeyed to *Nain*, a village of Galilee, and raised a dead man, "the only son of his widowed mother." *Screen*

Wine at Cana: the changing of the water into wine during the wedding at Cana, "the first of the signs by which Jesus revealed his glory and led his disciples to believe in him" (John 2.11). *Arecibo's Dish*

wired for bliss: programmed for happiness. See Menzel and D'Aluisio, *Robo sapiens* 76: A face robot developed at the Science University of Tokyo possesses "shape-memory actuators that move like muscles" and that create "expressions beneath the robot's silicon skin." *The Atom of the Word*

wold: an upland plain or hill. *When I Was a Foetus*

the Word that we parole: Christ, the manifested "Holy One" that we not only *indicate* as word (from the French term *parole*), the coded signifier of our faith, but also *express*—through humankind's redemptive release from Nature—as the unfettered Spirit of His circumcised heart. See Murray, *The Spirit of Christ* 126-27. *Orphan*

world-egg: "the philosophical egg of the medieval natural philosophers, the vessel from which, at the end of the *opus alchymicum*, the homunculus emerges, that is, the Anthropos, the spiritual, inner, and complete man [. . .]" (Jung, *The Archetypes and the Collective Unconscious* 293). *The Atom of the Word*

wormhole: in hyperspace, amid endlessly spawning universes, a crosscut from one place and time to another. *Heart of Flesh*

A worm in the ashes: here, not just the common, curling earthworm, but also conflated alchemical symbols—both the tail-eating Ouroboros and the "fiery serpent" of the soul (Jung, *Psychology and Alchemy* 166). *When I Was a Foetus*

wound in the cast: wrapped in the elaborate shroud of the mummified centuries. The metaphor is also theatrical—Christ leads, even as He indwells, His coheirs in the paschal drama of salvation. *Citizen of the Cosmos*

Wrestlers at Penuel: in Gen. 32.24-26, Jacob and the "man" who tested him and with whom he strove "till daybreak." Evidently, Jacob's opponent was "Jehovah, the preincarnate Christ." See *Thru the Bible with J. Vernon McGee*, vol. 1 (Nashville: Nelson, 1981) 133. *Reuben's Mandrakes*

Yahweh's Cheshire grinning: Cosmos, star, planet, species, the individual speaker himself—all shall, like the Cheshire cat in Lewis Carroll's *Alice's Adventures in Wonderland*, wink out. *Cinderdust*

Yahweh's hieroglyph, heron on the wing: Here, with its cleansing powder-down feathers, the *heron*, a variant *avis Hermetis*, becomes a substitute for *Yahweh's* iconic dove, the latter bird having been returned by God to Noah, after the Deluge, "with a newly plucked olive leaf in her beak" (Gen. 8.11). *Reuben's Mandrakes*

Yahweh's obelisk: a four-sided stone monument that tapers toward a pyramidal top—not a rejected idol, as in Exod. 23.24 and Hos. 10.2, but Jacob's "sacred pillar" instead (Gen. 28.18). *Arecibo's Dish*

yod: both the tenth letter of the Hebrew alphabet and the Gnostic symbol of the indivisible point, i.e., of the "perfect and indivisible man." Thus, "The Original Man, Adam, signifies the small hook at the top of the letter Yod [']" (Jung, *Aion* 218n136). The word rhymes with "wood." *A Single Day*

zero-G: a popular term for zero gravity, the condition of weightlessness that "results from a balance between the earth's gravitational pull and the inertia of a spacecraft [. . .]. Zero gravity is floating without having to pay the consequences—a strange and sublime experience that is at once bizarre and immensely enjoyable, a relaxed, slow-motion state in which all of the earth-bound rules have been broken" (Allen and Martin, *Entering Space* 65). *Planet of the Body*

Zion: Mount *Zion*, the site of "that new Jerusalem which is coming down out of heaven [. . .]" (Rev. 3.12) at End-time. *Arecibo's Dish*

Zone of Avoidance: near the plane of the Milky Way, the region of the night sky obscured by dust and stars. *Planet of the Body*

www.ingramcontent.com/pod-product-compliance
Lightning Source LLC
Chambersburg PA
CBHW081351080526
44588CB00016B/2460